How to Pass
Graduate
Psychometric Tests

Essential preparation for numerical and
verbal ability tests plus personality
questionnaires

4th edition

Mike Bryon

KoganPage

LONDON PHILADELPHIA NEW DELHI

Publisher's note

Every possible effort has been made to ensure that the information contained in this book is accurate at the time of going to press, and the publishers and author cannot accept responsibility for any errors or omissions, however caused. No responsibility for loss or damage occasioned to any person acting, or refraining from action, as a result of the material in this publication can be accepted by the editor, the publisher or the author.

First Published as *Graduate Recruitment Tests* in 1994
Reprinted in 1994 as *How to Pass Graduate Recruitment Tests*
Reprinted with revisions in 1995
Reprinted in 1996, 1997, 1998
Second Edition as *How to Pass Graduate Psychometric Tests* in 2001
Reprinted in 2002 (twice), 2003, 2005
Third Edition in 2007
Reprinted 2008, 2009
Fourth Edition in 2011

120 Pentonville Road	1518 Walnut Street, Suite 1100	4737/23 Ansari Road
London N1 9JN	Philadelphia PA 19102	Daryaganj
United Kingdom	USA	New Delhi 110002
www.koganpage.com		India

© Mike Bryon, 1994, 2001, 2007, 2011

The right of Mike Bryon to be identified as the author of this work has been asserted by him in accordance with the Copyright, Designs and Patents Act 1988.

ISBN   978 0 7494 6209 3
E-ISBN   978 0 7494 6210 9

British Library Cataloguing in Publication Data

A CIP record for this book is available from the British Library.

Library of Congress Cataloging-in-Publication Data

Bryon, Mike.
   How to pass graduate psychometric tests : essential preparation for numerical and verbal ability tests plus personality questionnaires / Mike Bryon. – 4th ed.
      p. cm.
   ISBN 978-0-7494-6209-3 – ISBN 978-0-7494-6210-9   1. Employment tests–Study guides. 2. Psychometrics. I. Title.
   HF5549.5.E5B779 2011
   650.076–dc22   2010041805

Typeset by Graphicraft Ltd, Hong Kong
Printed and bound in India by Replica Press Pvt Ltd

Contents

4   **English usage, reading comprehension and critical reasoning** 128

5   **Answers and many explanations** 221

Preface

This book is intended for the graduate who needs to revise the fundamentals of English usage or maths or both before taking a psychometric test. Many of the sections start at an easy level, lead you through the key competencies and conclude with questions at the level you can expect in a real psychometric test.

Use it to stand head and shoulders above the crowd of other applicants. You will be one of the many tens of thousands to use these proven exercises and go on to pass the tests of some of the most successful UK companies in their annual graduate recruitment campaigns.

To excel is not simply a matter of intelligence but requires you to be sufficiently motivated to want to pass and to try hard. A determination to do well is easily the most important ingredient for success. Passing a psychometric test when there are many hundreds of other candidates depends on your arriving very well prepared. Use these exercises and realistic practice tests to build up speed, accuracy and confidence. Use the grammar and maths glossaries to revise essential fundamentals.

Everyone can pass these tests, but you should realize that some candidates need to prepare more than others. This book will suit the graduate who must first revise competencies he or she may have long forgotten or never mastered. Some will have to invest a considerable amount of time before they succeed in a test they may have previously failed.

If you are one of many thousands of candidates, then you may need to undertake a quite considerable amount of revision and use more material than is contained in this volume. These intensive competitions are a serious test of your determination, resilience and endurance – just the qualities employers are seeking, and virtues that you can develop and be justly proud of. Be prepared to make a quite considerable commitment in terms of time and effort. Otherwise, risk coming a rather poor second. Throughout, I have suggested suitable sources of further practice material in the Kogan Page testing series.

Your university course may not have prepared you very well for an employer's psychometric test. The content may seem to you faulty or arbitrary. You may well question the validity of the whole exercise. You may consider some statements made to be factually incorrect. Many very able candidates spend too long on questions, thinking too deeply about them, and their score suffers accordingly. The science graduate or engineer may hate the fact that questions are to an extent deliberately ambiguous and that diagrams and scales can be distorted, especially on computer-administered tests. It is common for graduates to feel resentment about having to take a test.

All these concerns are entirely valid but they will not help. The test author has designed the question so that there is a correct answer. If the scale is distorted then the question is bound to contain the information you need to answer it correctly. Yes, the test may well contain controversial or factually incorrect statements. That is intentional, because they are testing you! Make sure you answer the question, not question the questions. They want the flexible worker, the employee who can follow instructions, the person who makes good decisions in a less than perfect world. They are looking for the candidate who can draw the best inference when there are gaps in the information available.

If you want that job and there is a test, then you have to do well in it. So, put aside any intellectual concerns. Accept the fact that you have to work at it in order to do well. You will not get all the questions right – and if you were told the answers, you would disagree with some of them. You just have to accept the situation or alternatively withdraw your application and go and do something else. The best-scoring candidates put aside any concerns; they see the test as an opportunity to prove to the employer just how good they really are. Make sure that you adopt this winning mindset.

You may find the exercises in this book testing, boring, painful even. Unfortunately, it has to be so. To pass many psychometric tests, you have to revise your mental arithmetic and concern yourself with correct English usage. If this book did not help you do this, then it would be failing you. You must also think carefully about the features of your personality that will appeal most to a particular company and be well practised in the interpretation of data and complex passages. The aim of this book is to provide a source of practice that allows you to perfect these essential test-taking skills.

This completely revised fourth edition contains close to 600 practice questions, an expanded chapter on personality questionnaires, a section on graduate assessment centres and, in response to readers' requests, harder and more reading comprehension, critical reasoning and data interpretation questions. These are all types of sub-test that have become increasingly fashionable since the publication of the first edition in 1994.

E-mail me at help@mikebryon.com if you use this book but need further guidance or advice. I will be happy to help. If you find a mistake, then do please take the trouble to inform me so that it can be removed at a future reprint. I and the editors have tried hard to keep them out but I am sure we have not got them all. If you find an error, try not to judge the book too harshly, as it most certainly does contain a lot of really useful practice material.

I wish you every success in the psychometric tests that you face and I dedicate this book to my children, Hope, Ella, Orlando and Allegra, and to my wife, Lorenza.

CHAPTER 1

Graduate psychometric tests

> I have been accepted by Procter & Gamble for a graduate position, so after 60 applications the search for a job is finally over. I am due to start work in October, which gives me time to go travelling, so I have booked a trip to the Far East, travelling to China, Vietnam, Cambodia, Thailand and ending in Singapore. It's scary to imagine but I am actually going to work.
>
> (A graduate candidate)

Psychometric tests are multiple-choice or short-answer tests completed online or with paper and pen. Graduate candidates should concern themselves with two principal types: tests of ability and personality questionnaires. Both are designed by occupational psychologists to apply standardized scientific methods and statistical techniques to provide a numerical measurement of the extent to which you demonstrate a particular trait or set of traits. These tests are used in a host of applications: for example, to select people for redundancy, diagnose people's strengths and weaknesses, allocate staff to the most appropriate tasks, identify training need and recruitment.

In recruitment – and in graduate recruitment in particular – psychometric tests are competitions; there are invariably more applicants than positions. The ability tests are also tests of endurance. They comprise a series or battery of tests sat one after the other, often against tight constraints. To complete the whole battery can take a number of hours and when you finish, you should feel worn out. I say 'should' because you have to apply yourself and really go for it if you are going to show your full potential and stand out from the crowd.

As a graduate you are bound to come across these tests in your search for work. If you are making a whole series of applications to most or all of the graduate recruitment campaigns, then it is likely that you will sit the same test a number of times.

The challenge of open and fair recruitment

A lot of good candidates are put off by tests and a lot more candidates fail to show their true potential in them. Test authors and employers go to considerable lengths to reassure us that their tests are objective and reliable and that they afford the selection of candidates with the potential to succeed in the given career or position.

From an employer's perspective, recruitment is a notoriously difficult business. Bad decisions and bad recruitment practice carry risks of damaging a business and may be open to legal challenge. To attract good applicants, many employers advertise their vacancies widely. To help to scrutinize large numbers of applicants objectively, employers use tools such as psychometric tests.

You, the candidate, will naturally try to get the best possible score and cover up any area of weakness when taking a test. The test author on the other hand must produce a test that offers as an objective an assessment of a candidate's ability while the candidate is trying to distort the outcome.

All tests should be recognized as less than perfect. This is because before a test can predict potential job performance, there first has to be a set of criteria against which to assess each candidate. However, job performance is a complex tapestry of factors and influences that is very hard to quantify numerically. Tests therefore risk attributing to the workplace too simplistic a set of performance indicators. Things are made more complex by the fact that their content – the questions – do not exactly measure the behavioural traits under investigation and inadvertently measure traits that are irrelevant to the post.

The introduction of cut-off points to reduce the number of people who pass through to the next stage in a recruitment process adds to the imperfection. It is usual for a company to reject candidates who do not beat a particular score. Alternatively, they fix an upper limit on the number of applicants allowed through. Such cut-off points create problems because they result in the rejection of many candidates who have the potential to do the job. The fact that tests are unavoidably imperfect also means that they will inadvertently overestimate the potential of some candidates who will be allowed through to the next stage.

It is important that you realize that when test authors talk about the objectivity of their test, they mean something quantifiably different from the objectivity obtained in the natural sciences. By 'objective' they mean that their test is more objective than alternative recruitment and selection methods. They might mean, for example, that their test is more reliable at predicting job performance than, say, an interview.

The maximum benefit of practice in ability tests

Taking a psychometric test is not a matter of simply rolling up your sleeve and putting up with the discomfort of the needle while the scientist takes a sample. There is no ambiguity attached to a blood-type classification; there is very little prospect of its changing according to the circumstances on the day on which the sample was taken. The objectivity of psychometric tests is quantifiably different. They are at best only indicators of potential. Had you not been suffering from a cold, had you been more familiar with the test conditions, been less nervous, better practised in mental arithmetic, not made that silly mistake... then you might have been classified differently. You might have passed something that, in the event, you failed.

Psychometric tests lack the certainty associated with the natural sciences. Accordingly, you, the subject, have considerable influence over the outcome. To a large extent the result will come down to the approach you take and how much you prepare.

Everyone, if they practise, can improve their test score. You can improve your score in every sort of test, even in a test where the questions are randomly selected so that they are different each time. The more interesting issue is not 'Can I improve my score?' but 'Can I improve my score sufficiently to pass something I would otherwise have failed?' The answer for most candidates is a resounding 'yes'.

Practice is almost certain to ensure that the candidate who is otherwise likely to fail by only a few marks, passes. Candidates who have little previous experience of psychometric tests can through practice demonstrate a quite considerable improvement in their score. Typically, the biggest gains are achieved quickly, and then the rate of improvement slows.

Psychometric ability tests nearly always include numerical and English usage sub-tests. Depending on your graduate course of study, these are subjects you may not have studied for many years. Practice in advance of these challenges can most definitely mean the difference between pass and fail.

Finally, practice can help you become familiar with the often unusual manner in which these questions are posed. It can help build speed and accuracy and help deal with nervousness and improve accuracy.

How much and what kind of practice?

Practice works best with material that is as much like the real questions as possible. The employer should have sent you or directed you towards a description of the test and in many cases a source of practice questions. Study this information carefully and seek out much more, and harder, practice material that closely resembles it.

It is best if you undertake two sorts of practice. You should:

1 Practise without time constraint and in an informal relaxed situation. The aim of this practice is that you realize the demands of the questions, understand how to approach them, and gain speed and confidence in your ability to answer them.

2 Practise on realistic questions against a strict time constraint and under as realistic test conditions as you can organize. The aim of this sort of practice is to get used to answering the questions under pressure. This will help you avoid mistakes and become faster.

Over weeks, aim to undertake a minimum of 12 hours' practice. If you can obtain sufficient practice material, then practise for as much as 20 hours. If you know that you need to make major gains in respect to your maths or English, then be prepared to commit significantly more time than this on a really quite major programme of work.

Your schedule of work should look something like this:

1 Study the test description.

2 Seek out as much free relevant material as you can.

3 Find further – and, especially, harder – practice questions from sources such as this and other titles in the Kogan Page testing series.

4 Go through practice questions at your own pace.

5 Set yourself a realistic practice test against a strict time limit.

6 Score your test and spend time understanding where you went wrong.

7 Undertake more practice without time constrictions, concentrating on the types of questions that you got wrong in your first practice test.

8 Sit further practice tests under strict timed conditions.

9 Repeat stage 7 as required.

If you are having any difficulty obtaining sufficient practice material or material of a certain type, then by all means contact me at help@mikebryon.com . If I know of any, then I will be more than happy to suggest sources.

> You will find free practice tests (you have to register at the first two sites) at www.shl.com, www.PSL.co.uk, www.mypsychometrictests.com and www.mikebryon.com. Be aware, however, that these examples serve only to introduce the style of questions, and the questions in the real test may be quite a bit harder.

Test-taking strategies

Each kind of test requires a slightly different strategy. However, the following points about the approach that you should adopt are universal in that they apply to all psychometric tests of ability.

The best-scoring candidates are the ones who arrive prepared. You should be fully aware of the demands of each sub-test before you attend on the day. Prior to the start of the test the computer program or test administrator will allow you to practise on a number of example questions and explain to you the question types and time allowed. You should already be entirely familiar with this information. It will all be available prior to the day on leaflets, websites or free practice test downloads. Your programme of practice should have included all types of sub-test involved.

It is critical that you approach the test with confidence in your abilities. The candidates who do best are the ones who look forward to the challenge and the opportunity to demonstrate their abilities. They realize they have nothing to lose if they do their very best and 'go for it'. Preparation is the key to this.

It is essential that you keep track of time during the test and manage how long you spend on any one question. You must keep going right up to the end and, if it is possible (a few tests do not allow you to review your past answers), take the last few minutes to check your work.

You have to practise at getting the balance between speed and accuracy right. In many tests, to do well you have to work really quickly while making the minimum of mistakes. In some tests, time is really tight. You have to work pretty quickly in the Citigroup online numerical test, and the time limit is also tough in the numerical test used by Deloitte.

Remember, the negative effect of being under pressure to work quickly may be made worse if, understandably, you suffer anxiety or nerves. Be prepared for the fact that a significant change in pace may occur between sub-tests. There are examples where you have plenty of time in one sub-test and then this is followed by another in which time is really tight. Getting the pace right and being able to respond to a new challenge during the test takes practice.

Everyone gets some answers wrong. In the vast majority of tests it is better that you risk getting some questions wrong, so do attempt every question rather than double-check every answer and be told that you have run out of time before you have finished.

If you hit a difficult section or question, don't lose heart – just keep going. You may well find that you come to a section of questions in which you can excel.

Educated guessing is often worthwhile and worth practising. If you are unsure of the answer to a multiple-choice test, consider all the suggested answers and try ruling some of them out as wrong. That way you can reduce the number of suggested answers from which to guess and, hopefully, increase your chance of guessing correctly. It is unlikely to help your score if you simply guess from the suggested answers in a random fashion. This is because many tests penalize wrong answers or unanswered questions. To best manage penalties for wrong or unanswered questions, you need to perfect time management during the test, and when you cannot answer the question, then exercise educated guessing.

In numerical tests, practise estimating answers. In some instances you can modify the sum to make it a more convenient, faster calculation and then look to the suggested answers to identify the correct one.

A summary of research findings

A study of some of the literature on the effects of coaching highlighted the following findings. I summarize them so that you can make your own assessment as to the likely benefit of practice and better understand the principal issues believed to determine the value of practice.

- Everyone can improve their score if they practise.

- Individuals with incomplete educational backgrounds are likely to benefit most from coaching.

- Those who have no, or little, previous experience of tests show an improvement in performance about twice that shown by those who have taken a test before.

- Improvements in scores are obtained by experiencing material similar to that which occurs in the real test.

- Practice with similar material under realistic test conditions produces the best results.

- Most of the improvement is gained quickly; then the rate of improvement slows.

- The effects of test coaching appear highly specific in that there is little transfer of benefit to other types of test.

- Big individual differences are found in the effect of coaching.

- Greatest improvement in test performance is obtained not from coaching but from education (over a long time-frame).

- Graduates who have not studied maths or English language for a number of years can significantly improve their test scores through practice in these important types of sub-test.

If you are invited to a graduate assessment centre

BT PROFESSIONAL SERVICES ASSESSMENT DAY

BT has outsourced recruitment to their professional services (PS) division to Accenture. If you reach the assessment day stage then you will meet graduates and managers from PS.

The day will comprise an analysis exercise, interview, 1:1 exercise and group exercise.

If you are invited to an assessment centre, the best approach is to set out to enjoy the day. The organizers should do absolutely everything they can to make you feel at ease, and you can look forward to the chance to meet other candidates and representatives of the company. Yes, it will be mentally challenging and tiring, but attend determined to give it your best shot and that way you will maximize your chances of coming out of the day with a job offer. Be sure to attend armed with the benefits of a careful look at the organization overall, the section in which you would like to be placed and the position for which you have applied.

The time you spend at the centre will vary between recruitment campaigns. The experience may also vary slightly between candidates attending on the same day because some will, for example, undertake the interview first, followed by a written exercise, while others will undertake the written assignment first and then the interview. Things are organized in this way to manage resources efficiently and to reduce the time you spend hanging around waiting your turn. Organizations will inform you of an outline of what your day at the centre will comprise. You can glean a lot of very useful information from what you are sent, especially any information about the competencies to be examined. Read between the lines and you will be able to decide on the best approach to take.

The most important thing to take with you when you attend the centre is suitable ID. For reasons of test security, administrators will want to be able to confirm that no one is impersonating you and attending on your behalf. Read carefully and follow the instructions on your invitation and contact the organizers if you have any questions. They will provide you with everything you need or are allowed in terms of pens, scrap paper, calculators and so on. It would be a big mistake to arrive late for your appointment, so locate the centre and make sure you can find it with time to spare.

The group exercise or role play

The topic or topics you are assigned to discuss vary from company to company, but you will find that group exercises are fundamentally similar in that you will be one of number of candidates and you must engage in consensual discussion.

Preparation time

Group exercises start with time to prepare. During the preparation time, list points that you feel are very important and make sure that these come up in the discussion. Make sure that you identify the objectives of the exercise. Don't worry if someone raises one of your points before you have the chance to make it; just contribute to its discussion and help develop the issue. You most likely will be told not to appoint a chairperson. Aim to play to your strengths. Use the data the organizers give you to work out some relevant figures (you should include figures even if maths is not your thing).

It is vital to listen to others. The organizers will be looking to see if your input helps to move the group forward, and whether you help the group to achieve its objectives.

In some cases you will be given a great deal of briefing information – almost more than you can read in the time allowed. If this is the case, review the material quickly and keep your notes very brief. You might decide on an assessment tool to help you deal with the briefing papers; examples include SWOT and PEST analyses (of strengths, weaknesses, opportunities, threats; and political, social, economic, technological factors). Another commonly used tool is the spider diagram, which is great for speed, recall and the emphasis of connections. Prepare these tools and think through these strategies before the day.

If you find that you do not have enough time to read all the background material, then decide what you want to say and use the time you have to make absolutely sure you have sufficient evidence to back up your planned comments. Don't forget to include figures.

You are likely to be briefed as a group, and the other group members are the people with whom you will discuss the topics. If it is appropriate and the opportunity presents itself, take the trouble to get to know some of them. This will really help with any nervousness you may suffer. You will find it much easier to have a constructive conversation with someone you have talked to before.

The discussion

The discussion will be observed and notes taken by the assessors. It may even be recorded on video. Push all this out of your mind as much as possible and keep your thoughts on the group, its objective and the discussion.

Try to avoid taking notes during the exercise. If you really must take notes, keep them extremely brief – just one-word reminders. You do not want the invigilators to notice that you are looking down at notes, you want them to notice lots of eye contact and nods in agreement and to conclude that you can listen and have understood the significance of the contribution of others, for example by modifying your position to take account of their contribution.

If you can, and the opportunity presents itself, speak first so that you make the first impression and demonstrate drive. Don't worry if your position is entirely different from everyone else's; you are being assessed on how you make your case, not what case you are making. So set out to make as good a case as you can for the view that you are representing, but also point out its weaknesses. Be enthusiastic even when discussing what might seem very mundane issues.

Be assertive in getting your points across, but be very careful not to stray into language that could be taken as aggressive. Listen as well as talk. Do make lots of eye contact and do nod in agreement, but don't shake your head or demonstrate your disagreement through body language. Consider making explicit reference to how you have modified your case to take into account the contributions of others. Do this by, for example, offering supportive summaries of others' contributions and then adding a further relevant point of your own.

Recognize the talents and merit in other people's contribution without diminishing your own. Use 'us' and 'we' to emphasize the collective purpose. Suggest criteria to clarify and evaluate the project. Help draw out quieter candidates by creating the space for them to speak by helping to ensure that everyone has a say. Show decisiveness and leadership qualities but avoid adopting the role of chairperson.

Don't take criticism personally. Don't start or get sucked into an argument, but in the unlikely event that one occurs, try to help make peace between the parties. This is important and a point on which many otherwise good candidates fail, so be sure to show empathy and go out of your way to resolve tension or disputes that arise between the other parties.

Take account of others' contributions and be prepared to adopt the suggestions of others over your own, as this will be taken as an indication of your willingness to support another's project, of flexibility and of a talent in the building of relationships. Be constructive in your contributions and be supportive of others in your group.

Keep your contributions to the point and spell out the relevance if you refer to something not immediately significant to the issue under discussion. Remember to make absolutely sure you have sufficient evidence to back up what you plan to say and include plenty of figures. The aim of everything you contribute should be to move the group towards the objectives of the exercise.

Self-evaluation of your performance

It is common for you to be asked to complete a self-assessment of your performance at an assessment centre. Take this exercise seriously as it is often scored and counts towards your overall mark. If appropriate, comment on both what you learnt from it and on how you might improve were you to attend the event or take the exercise again. Keep your self-criticism positive but be sure it is genuine. You might comment on, for example, how productive your relationship building was, the impact of your communication, or how the group could have better developed the assignment.

Many candidates find critical self-evaluation a challenge; we are all so used to hiding our weaknesses and promoting our strengths. But realize that otherwise very strong candidates fail because they have not been open enough about their weaknesses and have not taken the opportunity to describe the strategies they have devised to address them.

Presentations

There is a lot you can do before the day to prepare for a presentation.

Plan something to say on core issues relevant to most subjects

Every sector of industry has issues that are relevant to pretty well every scenario. They depend on the industry, of course, but might include recent legislation, the environment, health and safety, equality of opportunity, inclusiveness of people with all types of disabilities and social inclusion generally. There are bound to be cross-cutting themes relevant to the organization to which you have applied, so research them. The opportunity may arise for you to refer to these issues and gain valuable points.

Decide in advance how you might structure your presentation

You are unlikely to know the subject of your presentation until a short time before you have to make it, but this does not mean that you cannot do some preparation on the possible structure you intend to use. In the introduction you may want to summarize what you intend to go on to say and then in your conclusion review what you have said. There are some very good publications on the making of successful presentations; they may be worth a look.

You might decide to start by stating succinctly the assignment and go on to describe why addressing the issue is useful or necessary. If appropriate you could then review the file material (relating to people, budget or rules) or background. Headings after that point might include Actions, Recommendations, Alternatives and Conclusion. Do not forget that it is essential that you show enthusiasm throughout.

Practise getting your timing right

You may not yet know how long you will have to present, but all the same it is worth practising how much you can say effectively in the usual time slots allocated in these exercises. On the day you will be allocated something between 10 and 20 minutes and you do not want to finish short or overrun. To get it right you need to have some experience of how long it will take to present a series of points with impact. Try to say too much or too little and you may end up disappointed with your presentation. Listen to a few public speakers on the radio, for example, and study how they make a point with impact and how long it takes them. You do not want to find yourself unable to cover all the points you planned to make and to be told to stop before you have made your concluding remarks.

The briefing and preparation time

You are often given a number of subjects from which to choose and are always provided with a briefing pack on the subject and told the time you have to prepare your presentation. Don't make the mistake of thinking you have to comment on all the subjects, including the ones you did not select. So, at the briefing, get absolutely clear in your mind the nature of the assignment and if in doubt ask someone for clarification. Be warned that it is common for the amount of time allowed for studying the background papers to be very tight. These events are sometimes organized so that the time allowed for reading the papers and preparing your presentation are combined, so be very careful not to spend too much time reading the papers and finding yourself with insufficient time to prepare your presentation.

Be sure to present the difficulties as well as the advantages of your approach to the topic. Often you are asked to provide something original on the subject. Even if you are not specifically asked to do this, it may be worth offering a novel aspect to your presentation and then going on to examine the benefits and challenges to this aspect. Don't forget to identify it as an original contribution. The relevance of everything you say should be clear or be explained. In practice, the invigilators don't so much care what you decide on but judge you on how you explain, justify and criticize it.

Once you have decided what to say, settle on your structure, make clear legible notes to which you can refer when making the presentation, and resolve to keep to them. Allocate an amount of time to each part of your presentation. Do not try to write out verbatim what you hope to cover. Even if you could manage it in the time allowed, the exercise is not one of you having to read your essay out loud. Instead, try numbering your points and commit these numbers and key words belonging to the points to memory. Try labelling them with one-word reminders and memorizing these. Try anything that works for you and will help you recall the points you want to make without excessive reference to your notes.

Remember to work quickly, as you may find you have very little time to prepare for your presentation.

Your presentation

Nerves aside, your presentation is likely to be as good or bad as your preparation, both before the day and during the preparation time. The invigilators are not expecting a polished public perform-ance, but do be sure to speak clearly, make eye contact and try to keep reference to your notes to a minimum. Do think on your feet and adapt what you say as you speak, then revert back to your structure. Keep an eye on the time and try as much as possible to keep to the limits you set for speaking on each part of your presen-tation. If you find yourself going over time, drop some points. As already said, it is more important to deliver a timely presentation than be asked to stop before you have reached your conclusions. You are very likely to get the opportunity to raise further points and add details in the question and answer session that follows.

Follow-up questions or discussion

In these exercises it is common for more time to be spent answering questions and discussing what you said with the invigilator than you spent making your presentation. It will help if you think of this time more as a brainstorming session than a cross-examination. So approach it with an open, curious mind rather than risk being perceived as defensive. During questions, the invigilators may follow up your response and keep asking follow-up questions until they feel they have the measure of you. At some point they will have decided whether you have made the grade, but they may still keep asking questions until you run out of things to say. Don't let this undermine your self-confidence and don't take offence. When the next line of questioning begins, it's a fresh start, a new line of enquiry, and you should have a different line of responses. Avoid falling back on a previous response (that is, avoid repeating yourself). At all times make sure your response is relevant to the question and the line of enquiry. Listening skills are as important here as they are in the group exercise. Expect there to be one person who leads the questions and one or more others who mainly observe and take notes.

Self-assessment

If you are required to complete a self-assessment of your performance in the presentation exercise then take it seriously and complete it to the best of your ability; a score of what you write may feature as a part of your overall assessment. (Refer back to the comments on self-evaluation above.)

Written exercises

Overview

These are tests of your ability to handle information, organize it and communicate in writing. You will be presented with a file of papers that provide information on a subject. They may include conflicting information that you have to evaluate and make recommendations about. Your task is to analyse the papers and prepare a note that builds a balanced and convincing case. To do this you will need to compare and contrast the options, using the stated criteria or proposing your own, and explain convincingly the reasons for your recommendation. These exercises are nearly always completed on a computer, so make sure your keyboard skills are up to scratch. They look at how well you can structure an argument and examine a number of options, recommending one. It does not so much matter which option you recommend as how you back up your recommendation.

Planning in advance

Again, you can undertake some useful preparation before the day. One thing to consider is the style of approach that you adopt. This decision will depend in part on your background and your strengths; it is obvious that you should play to these. It should also be dependent on the role for which you are applying. By this I mean that if you are applying for a role in business then adopt a business style of report writing, with an executive summary stating the recommendation and summarizing the whole document, followed by the main body and then the conclusion. If you are applying to an academic institution, then a university style of report may be more appropriate and you should, if you can, adopt an elegant, fluid, readable written style. Research on the internet the style of reports and publications used in the organization or industrial sector in which it operates and, if you are confident to do so, adopt this style in the written exercise. That way you will appear well suited to the position. If producing a written document is really not your thing, consider using (but not excessively) bullet points and underlined headings to help convey your message. Illustrate points, where applicable – they will be far more convincing. If you find that you have not included numbers in your notes, then you have probably not done as well as you could, so, where practical, back up and provide numerical evidence for what you say. Many organizations are looking for you to provide evidence of the case or point you make, so refer to figures or passages in the background paper and remember to source references.

Before the day it may be useful to give thought to analytical tools or processes to which you might refer or use in the exercise. Some have already been mentioned above, including SWOT and PEST. Consider whether there are any core issues to which you might make reference in your paper that are applicable to most issues in the industrial sector to which you are applying. Look at reports and studies on the internet to identify possible issues. They might include, for example, equality of opportunity, reaching the hard to reach or challenging members of our society, or the contributions and/or threats technological advances might bring.

A common question asked is how much should I write? The answer is that, within reason, what matters is not how much you write but what you write. Some assignments stipulate the extent expected, others do not. When no extent is indicated, set out to write enough to get the job done well. Don't write without good purpose, and take care to use the correct grammar, spelling and punctuation. Write too much and you increase the risk of errors and have less time to find any errors you may have made.

The briefing and preparation time

When you come to take the assignment it is very likely that you will be briefed on the exercise and provided with background or briefing papers. You may have a lot of information to go through and the time allowed to complete this part of the task may be tight. Be sure not to get caught out by the time limit. You need to be clear about the aim of the exercise as explained to you and, first and foremost, use the time allowed to obtain the information necessary to serve the objective of the assignment. Then set about deciding the line to take in your paper and the structure that you will adopt.

The written assignment itself

Much of what you have done during your education and working career to date will serve you well in a written exercise. Take confidence from the fact that you have the skill to succeed in this assessment and apply what you have prepared before the day and during the briefing and preparation time. Although the written assignment is almost certainly to be administered on a PC, think back to the written exams at school or university for an idea of what to expect and insight into the best approach. Start with a note of the structure that you have decided to adopt and then use your time to implement that plan. Take care over grammar and spelling. Remember the invigilators are looking to see how well you can structure an argument and examine a number of options, recommending one. Where appropriate, use illustrations to make your points; back up what you say with figures; consider rather than quote from the background information, paraphrasing it or restating the passage in your own words. Demonstrate your ability at handling numerical information by offering clear, succinct restatements of relevant data in the background information. Remember to reference sources. Be convincing while remaining impartial and objective.

The interview

Typically the interview lasts 45 minutes and is conducted by a panel comprising HR professionals and managers from the department or graduate programme to which you are applying. Expect a series of questions examining the extent to which you can demonstrate the competencies essential to the role. You will be expected to illustrate when and where you have displayed these competencies. Your examples can refer to your past work study, home life or hobbies. Expect follow-up questions that examine your objectives, the outcome and perhaps how you might have done things better.

Prepare by identifying each competency's link with the role, and things you have done in the past that demonstrate you hold that competency. When using an example of something you have done, use each example only once (as you won't get credit for repeating examples). If you use several examples you will appear a rounded interesting candidate and avoid the possibility that the interviewers give you credit for only one thing.

Next imagine possible follow-up questions and start thinking about how you might respond to them. An interview is an oral exam – you are judged on what you say in response to the questions asked of you. Start your preparation if it helps by writing notes on what you want to say but, and this is important, remember that you must speak your answers and you are not allowed to hand in an essay. So memorize your notes but then put them away and get practising by speaking.

You will not be allowed to make a speech that you have prepared. An interview is a conversation. That conversation could go in a number of directions and you must listen and respond to what the interviewers say. You must refer to all your positive experiences and each of your many qualities in answer to a relevant question asked of you. You must learn to adjust your answer in response to the question and make sure that your answer is to the point. You may then be asked follow-up questions based on what you have said and you will have to provide a clear, relevant answer to them.

It can be a difficult balance; first you must obviously listen to the question, decide on an appropriate reply and deliver that reply clearly and concisely. You may then have to justify what you have said or illustrate it further in response to follow-up questions. To become good at interview you have to practise, but it is important that you undertake the right sort of practice. Start by preparing answers to the following questions and follow-up questions and also do read one of the many interview books such as *Great Answers to Tough Interview Questions* by Martin Yates published by Kogan Page.

Can you tell us about an occasion when you have seen a difficult job through to its successful end?

Possible follow-up questions:

　Can you tell us about another example?
　How might you have done things better?

Can you describe a situation when you have motivated others to achieve something challenging?

Possible follow-up questions:

　How did you feel about the outcome of this?
　Can you think of another example?
　How might you have done things differently had one of the people involved been disabled or if the person did not speak English?

Can you tell us of an occasion when you have shown a commitment to maintaining your knowledge?

Possible follow-up questions:

Can you tell us of something you are doing now to maintain your knowledge?

What more do you think you could be doing?

When have you worked with others to resolve a problem?

Possible follow-up question:

How did you inform your supervisor of this situation?

Can you give an example of when a policy of equality of opportunity was beneficial?

Possible follow-up questions:

Can you think of any other reason why equality of opportunity is important?

What does equal opportunities mean to you?

In practical terms how can you apply an equal opportunities policy?

Can you tell us about an occasion when you have completed a task following written procedures?

Possible follow-up question:

Can you describe another occasion?

Can you describe to us a situation where you had to explain something to a group of people?

Possible follow-up question:

How would you have dealt with this situation if one of the group could not speak English or was hearing impaired?

Can you describe a situation where you have had to change the way you did something?

Possible follow-up question:

Can you tell us how you how you felt in general about the change?

If you suffer from a disability

If your ability to undertake an assessment could be adversely affected by a disability then speak to or e-mail the recruitment team of the employer and seek their advice on how your requirements can best be accommodated. Provide full details of your condition and be clear on the special arrangements you require.

You may be allowed extra time or a test reader or someone to record your answers. Braille or large text versions of the test may be made available.

It is reasonable to expect that your requirements are given proper consideration and wherever possible are accommodated. Evidence of your condition may be required. Be sure to raise your needs at an early stage in order that the organizers have time to accommodate them and you have sufficient time to obtain any formal proof of your condition that they may require.

If you face a graduate assessment many years after leaving college

If it is some or many years since you studied, then a graduate psychometric assessment may well present a number of specific hurdles. The first thing to do is to review examples of each type of question and assignment that makes up the assessment you face and make an honest assessment of which of these components represent for you the greatest challenge.

To demonstrate your full potential (and well before sitting the test) you will need to begin a programme of revision. Start with the aspects of the test that you feel you are least good at.

You may need to set aside a fairly considerable amount of time for revising the demands of the verbal and numerical sub-tests. Ideally over a number of months, aim at 10 hours' practice a week. Making the necessary commitment will demand discipline and determination as the time spent practising will at times seem tedious and frustrating.

Work to redevelop a good exam technique. This demands a balance between speed and accuracy. Some very good candidates will need to unlearn a thoughtful, considered approach to issues. You can actually think too deeply or take too few risks in a test. Practise realistic questions under the pressure of time. Where appropriate look to the suggested answers for clues and practise informed guessing (where you can eliminate some of the suggested answers and then guess from those that remain).

On a positive note, practice should afford you a marked improvement in your performance. Your work history may have prepared you well for many of the assessments.

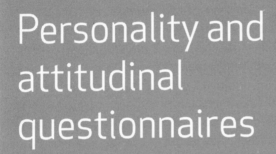

CHAPTER 2

Personality and attitudinal questionnaires

Psychometric Services Ltd (PSL) produces a whole range of online and pen and paper personality questionnaires with titles including:

Occupational Personality Inventory
Dynamic Personality Questionnaire
Motivational Questionnaire
Customer Service Questionnaire
Advanced Sales Questionnaire

You may well come across the PSL questionnaires (and ability tests). PSL has a very extensive client list, including for example Cadbury Schweppes, HMV, Lloyds TSB and Toyota, to name but a few of the many hundreds of national and international companies PSL has as its clients.

Every organization will require graduate applicants to complete a bundle of forms. Very often these include some type of questionnaire. It will comprise a series of questions to which you must indicate your attitude. You are required, for example, to indicate whether you agree or disagree, agree or disagree strongly, or neither agree nor disagree with each statement. Increasingly these questionnaires are completed online, but they are still sometimes done with pen and paper.

It is common for the same issue to be returned to at a number of points in the questionnaire and even the same question to be repeated. The test author uses this quite annoying strategy to investigate the consistency of your responses.

It is important that you realize these questionnaires are used to filter out candidates whose responses suggest they will not fit well in the organization's preferred style of working. Many, many candidates complete them in haste and give far too little thought to their function and significance. From now on, take these questionnaires far more seriously. They may well represent the stage in the recruitment process at which the largest numbers of applicants are rejected.

Personality questionnaires in which there is strictly speaking no right or wrong answer

Most of the questions in personality questionnaires do not have a definitive right or wrong answer. The preferred answer depends on the company using them and the sort of profile of person it is looking for and the responses that it considers most suitable. You should therefore always answer these questions with the job role and organization at the fore of your mind. Allow me to illustrate the point with the following mini-questionnaire.

Practice for personality questionnaires

Below you will find five example personality questions repeated three times. You will answer the five questions three times. First consider and answer the example questions but do not refer to a particular organization or role.

When I cook a meal I prefer to follow the recipe exactly.	Agree	Disagree
I try to get others to do a job the way I think it should be done.	Agree	Disagree
I always try to include others in my plans.	Agree	Disagree
I try to strongly influence other people's actions.	Agree	Disagree
I find myself the dominant person in many social situations.	Agree	Disagree

Now answer the same questions again but imagine you were applying and want to work for a company needing 'a safe pair of hands': a candidate capable of handling difficult situations diplomatically.

When I cook a meal I prefer to follow the recipe exactly.	Agree	Disagree
I try to get others to do a job the way I think it should be done.	Agree	Disagree
I always try to include others in my plans.	Agree	Disagree
I try to strongly influence other people's actions.	Agree	Disagree
I find myself the dominant person in many social situations.	Agree	Disagree

Finally, answer the same questions but imagine yourself applying for a choice role that requires a person driven to succeed in a highly competitive 'dog eat dog' market in which success only comes to those prepared to work extremely hard and who are comfortable with a degree of risk.

When I cook a meal I prefer to follow the recipe exactly.	Agree	Disagree
I try to get others to do a job the way I think it should be done.	Agree	Disagree
I always try to include others in my plans.	Agree	Disagree
I try to strongly influence other people's actions.	Agree	Disagree
I find myself the dominant person in many social situations.	Agree	Disagree

Now compare your answers. On your second attempt you should have answered the questions very differently from the third. A company looking for 'a safe pair of hands' might prefer the person inclined to stick to the recipe. A diplomatic approach does not normally involve trying to strongly influence people or always getting others to do the job your way. This contrasts strongly with a company operating in a highly competitive market. Such a company might well prefer the person inclined not to follow the recipe, and could well be attracted to the dominant personality.

It may be that your first response to these questions, the response in which you did not have a role or organization in mind, is different again, but realize that if you answer these questions outside of the context – that is, without reference to the role and organization to which you are applying – then you may well be failing to present yourself in the best light and risk rejection at the first hurdle from a job you want.

All this does not mean that you should not answer these questionnaires truthfully. You should, and you should be prepared to make responses that you realize may not be the preferred responses. In any event, a handful of low-scoring responses are unlikely to result in your rejection. The point is that you should emphasize the bits of your personality that best fit the role and organization. This is no different from the way in which you might customize a CV, emphasizing particular attributes to best suit a particular career, or answer an interview question differently depending on the context.

Practice at 40 more personality questionnaire statements

Below you will find 40 typical examples of the sorts of questions that occur in personality questionnaires. You should be aware that in a real test the questionnaire is likely to be specific to a particular industrial sector or a particular grade of worker, or to investigate a particular trait in greater detail, whereas these practice questions are necessarily general to any role or sector and across many traits.

The statements are organized under headings of the principal categories of behaviour investigated by questionnaires. Use these questions to practise for a real questionnaire. Remember to keep to the fore of your mind the type of role and organization in which you would prefer to work. Practise being consistent in your responses. Obviously it is not possible for me to give a correct answer to these questions because it would depend on the role and organization to which you would like to apply. However, I have offered explanations of the sort of conclusion that might be drawn from your response.

A useful tip is that it is best to avoid too many 'neither agree nor disagree' responses in a real questionnaire as this could be taken to conclude that you find it difficult to commit yourself.

Also take care not to suggest that you have too many strongly held opinions. (This would only apply to a questionnaire that offered the option of responding 'agree strongly' or 'disagree strongly'.)

Usually, no time limit is applied to these questionnaires, so allow yourself as long as you wish to respond to the following:

S1   I sometimes let small things upset me more than they should.

Agree   Neither agree nor disagree   Disagree

S2   I do not find regulations and written procedures restrictive.

Agree   Neither agree nor disagree   .   Disagree

S3   It's human nature to be lazy whenever possible.

Agree   Neither agree nor disagree   Disagree

S4   Working life unavoidably involves dealing with the unforeseen.

Agree   Neither agree nor disagree   Disagree

S5   I would not describe myself as someone who worries too much about things.

Agree   Neither agree nor disagree   Disagree

S6   If you want to get ahead of your team-mates, then keep your cards close to your chest.

Agree   Neither agree nor disagree   Disagree

S7   I have a tendency to feel responsibility for things going on at work even if they are not a part of my job.

Agree   Neither agree nor disagree   Disagree

S8   In order to manage people well you have to watch over every detail.

Agree   Neither agree nor disagree   Disagree

S9   I find it hard to cope when a whole series of things go wrong.

Agree   Neither agree nor disagree   Disagree

S10   It is not always a matter of fun, and harmless, to be humorous at work.

Agree   Neither agree nor disagree   Disagree

S11 I try to be the dominant person when I am in a group.

Agree   Neither agree nor disagree   Disagree

S12 At work I get bored when I undertake familiar tasks.

Agree   Neither agree nor disagree   Disagree

S13 It is advisable to plan for the worst case even if this delays slightly the implementation of new products.

Agree   Neither agree nor disagree   Disagree

S14 I am only patient with people if they are polite and considerate.

Agree   Neither agree nor disagree   Disagree

S15 It is much more effective to communicate ideas orally than in writing.

Agree   Neither agree nor disagree   Disagree

S16 I can't rely on my own initiative and am much happier as a part of a team.

Agree   Neither agree nor disagree   Disagree

S17 It is normal that your working life should interfere with your busy social life.

Agree   Neither agree nor disagree   Disagree

S18 To succeed, one has to break with the past and experiment with the new.

Agree   Neither agree nor disagree   Disagree

S19 I can talk with ease about how I feel.

Agree   Neither agree nor disagree   Disagree

S20 I am more objective in the inferences that I draw than most people I know.

Agree   Neither agree nor disagree   Disagree

S21 Success follows a detailed understanding of the marketplace.

Agree   Neither agree nor disagree   Disagree

S22 What I do in my own time is none of my employer's business.

Agree   Neither agree nor disagree   Disagree

S23 I often suspect that people who appear friendly are in fact the opposite.

Agree   Neither agree nor disagree   Disagree

S24 I would rather work in a laboratory helping to invent something than in the sales team trying to sell it.

Agree   Neither agree nor disagree   Disagree

S25 I like people to invite me to join in with their activities.

Agree   Neither agree nor disagree   Disagree

S26 It is sometimes clever to make a sarcastic remark.

Agree   Neither agree nor disagree   Disagree

S27 If I worked in advertising I would rather be involved in the accounts of sportspeople or celebrities than in those of multi-national companies.

Agree   Neither agree nor disagree   Disagree

S28 Some tasks do not need to be done as carefully as others.

Agree   Neither agree nor disagree   Disagree

S29 You can have too many new initiatives, especially if, like buses, they all tend to come along at once.

Agree   Neither agree nor disagree   Disagree

S30 I find it hard to start a conversation with someone I do not know.

Agree   Neither agree nor disagree   Disagree

S31 I just can't see how a 'no-blame' culture can be good for business.

Agree   Neither agree nor disagree   Disagree

S32 I most definitely do not see my ideal role as one of providing counsel and impartiality.

Agree   Neither agree nor disagree   Disagree

S33 It is possible to demonstrate good manners in most but not all situations.

Agree   Neither agree nor disagree   Disagree

S34 I rarely have time to read it all but I like to be copied into all correspondence.

Agree   Neither agree nor disagree   Disagree

S35 It is far more important to be judged decisive than to be judged competent.

Agree   Neither agree nor disagree   Disagree

S36 Good leadership is about boldness far more than listening skills.

Agree   Neither agree nor disagree   Disagree

S37 I would not be discouraged by a set of stretching performance indicators against which I would be assessed.

Agree   Neither agree nor disagree   Disagree

S38 I work at my best when I can keep distractions to a minimum.

Agree   Neither agree nor disagree   Disagree

S39 I let others decide what to do.

Agree   Neither agree nor disagree   Disagree

S40 I absolutely refuse to accept failure.

Agree   Neither agree nor disagree   Disagree

Attitudinal questionnaires to which there is most definitely a wrong answer

You are most likely to come across an attitudinal questionnaire if you apply to, for example, a police or other emergency authority, or a public service organization generally.

This fast-growing part of the questionnaire market typically involves a mix of statements, many of which you and the employer will be in complete agreement over, but in among them will be a statement that probes your attitude towards, for example, honesty, colleagues, customer care, equality of opportunity, and health and safety.

With these questions it is quite possible for your application to be rejected on the basis of a single wrong response. This might occur if, for example, you agree with a statement that supports direct racial discrimination in the workplace or asserts that violent or gross misconduct is acceptable at work. More likely the questions will be subtle enough to require a pattern of wrong responses before a rejection is triggered.

Examples

Your response to these statements is very unlikely to differ depending on the company to which you are applying or the role in question. From the test-taker's perspective it is this feature that makes this type of questionnaire so different from the personality questionnaires. Consider the following 10 examples. Be careful when the statement involves a negative:

S1   I would not really consider it any of my business if I witnessed a colleague stealing company property.

Agree   Disagree

S2 At some point we all make mistakes and what counts is that we work together to correct them.

Agree   Disagree

S3 It's not obvious that people should refrain from using bad language at work.

Agree   Disagree

S4 You just know that there are some sorts of people that you are going to get on better with than others.

Agree   Disagree

S5 I am not the sort of person who lets things that upset me build up until I blow my top.

Agree   Disagree

S6 If it were not a condition of my contract of employment, then I might not agree to a request from my employer that I undertake a medical examination by a qualified doctor of medicine.

Agree   Disagree

S7 Someone who is off sick with a stress-related illness is unavoidably putting more stress on everyone else who has to go to work and do that person's job as well as their own.

Agree   Disagree

S8 Most employers expect employees to pay lip service to equality of opportunities but at the end of the day it is not going to help get the job done.

Agree   Disagree

S9 I have always been comfortable with being told what to do.

Agree   Disagree

S10 When I find that I have a different opinion from others I prefer
to end the discussion or to discuss something else.

Agree   Disagree

You will find a personality test comprising 130 practice questions in
The Graduate Psychometric Workbook and a further 100 practice
questions in *Ultimate Psychometric Tests*, both published by Kogan
Page.

Situational awareness tests

Situational awareness tests comprise a passage in which an
imaginary workplace situation is described. These tests then list
suggested responses to that situation. In the type of situational
awareness test given below, your task is to rank the suggested
responses as either the most appropriate, acceptable or less than
acceptable. Note that there are more suggested responses than
categories in which you can rank them. This means that you must
rank more than one response as the same category. Use only your
own best judgement and the information provided to decide the
rankings.

Identify as the most appropriate the response that you consider
is the best of those suggested. If you consider two or more of the
suggested responses the most appropriate then do not rank any
of the answers as A but instead rank them as B – acceptable. It is
possible that you do not consider any of the suggested responses
the most appropriate or acceptable, in which case do not rank any
of the answers as A or B. If you are unfamiliar with this style of test
then it might be worthwhile attempting the first question and then
reading the answer and explanation to it before attempting the
remaining questions.

To an extent the answer to these situations depends on your
preferred working style and the preferences of the organization to
which you are applying. Answers and explanations are provided
in Chapter 5, but take them as indicative rather than absolute, as

different organizations may judge the responses differently. To score your answers award yourself a maximum of 4 marks per question; one mark for each correct ranking you attribute to each suggested response.

Situation 1

You are entering the building where you work and find a man standing at the door. The door requires a pass to be placed over a pad before it opens. You use your pass to unlock the door. Without thinking you hold the door open for the man who enters with you and thanks you. He looks smart and business-like but you do not recognize him. This does not mean that he does not work in the building or should not be inside, as many people work there and you do not know them all. You decide to ask to see his security pass but he refuses and tells you that he works in security and that he does not have to show you his pass.

Rate the suggested responses as:

A. The most appropriate response
B. An acceptable response
C. A less than acceptable response

These are the suggested responses:

1 You would ask the person his name and go to your office and call security to check whether it is true that he works there.

2 You would politely insist that he shows you his pass.

3 You would offer to accompany him to the office of the security team so that they may confirm he works there.

4 You would let the matter drop.

| Your answer | 1 | 2 | 3 | 4 |

Situation 2

A colleague complains to you about the bad breath of a member of your team. On a few occasions you have noticed the problem yourself but decided against saying anything as you are aware of some personal difficulties that the individual faces.

Rate the suggested responses as:

A. The most appropriate response
B. An acceptable response
C. A less than acceptable response

These are the suggested responses:

1 You would quietly explain to your colleague the nature of the personal problems that the individual faces and ask your colleague to be more understanding.

2 You would resolve to raise the matter with the individual at the next team meeting and inform your colleague that you will handle it.

3 You would ask your colleague to say no more on the subject and do nothing.

4 You would meet privately with the member of your team, tell that person about the problem and ask that he or she does something about it.

Your answer   1   2   3   4

Situation 3

You receive a letter from a member of the public complaining that vehicles leaving your company's premises are taking a short cut along a cycle path and he fears that a cyclist might get injured or even killed.

Rate the suggested responses as:

A. The most appropriate response
B. An acceptable response
C. A less than acceptable response

These are the suggested responses:

1 You would reply thanking him for his letter and saying that you will circulate it within the organization to staff in appropriate positions.

2 You would reply stating that you agree entirely that this is a dangerous practice and that you will raise the matter at the first opportunity with all concerned and write again to inform him of what is decided.

3 You would reply explaining that as the premises overlook the cycle path you are sure the fact is already well known so you really don't think there is anything you can do.

4 You would reply suggesting that it would be more appropriate for him to take the matter up with the police as they are responsible for road safety.

| Your answer | 1 | 2 | 3 | 4 |

Situation 4

You were asked to try and sort out a failing project, the aim of which was to get more 16–18 year olds to remain in education. The first thing you had to address was the steering group, which comprised representatives of 12 organizations, all with competing agendas, priorities and interests. When you attended the first steering group's meeting you realized just how bad things were as each organization had been using its own system to collate results from its activities. This meant that you were presented with 12 different sets of data. The individuals who made up the steering group were highly influential but their morale was low and some declared that they were close to resigning from the group. Your manager explained to you that if this happened the project would have to close.

Rate the suggested responses as:

A. The most appropriate response
B. An acceptable response
C. A less than acceptable response

These are the suggested responses:

1 You would address the meeting and offer as compelling a case as possible for the representatives to support you in an attempt to turn things around.

2 You would ask members of the steering group to tell you how they think the project could be saved.

3 You would immediately set about agreeing with the representatives what is needed to turn the project around and negotiate with both your manager and the representatives to ensure that those resources were made available to the project.

4 You would undertake to collate the 12 sets of data and identify findings that can be inferred across the different sets of data.

   Your answer   1   2   3   4

Situation 5

You criticize a member of your staff for grammatical errors in a report and the individual denies being the author. You realize that you are mistaken but before you have a chance to say any more the individual concerned gets extremely angry and starts shouting and using bad language. The individual is shouting so loudly that you are sure others can hear what the person is saying.

Rate the suggested responses as:

A. The most appropriate response
B. An acceptable response
C. A less than acceptable response

Here are the suggested responses:

1 You would interrupt to tell the person to stop shouting and using bad language and say that when the person has calmed down you wish to speak to him or her. You would then turn away and leave the person

2 You would let the person have his or her say and then apologize and retract your criticism.

3 You would let the person finish and calmly tell him or her not to shout and swear and then you would apologize and retract your criticism.

4 You would interrupt to stop the person and explain that you wish to apologize for your error but that it is entirely unacceptable for the person to shout and use bad language and if he or she does not stop immediately you will walk away and discuss the matter with him or her later.

Your answer   1   2   3   4

Situation 6

The first year of the project has gone well; however, while you encourage your team members to take a moment to congratulate themselves you are well aware that it would be considerably harder to repeat the success in year 2. Your caution is based on the fact that the project's year 2 targets are many times higher than those of year 1 and your team will have to raise the game considerably if they are to repeat the success.

Rate the suggested responses as:

A. The most appropriate response
B. An acceptable response
C. A less than acceptable response

These are the suggested responses:

1 You would circulate an e-mail alerting the team to your concerns and your view that everyone will have to raise the game considerably if the targets for year 2 are to be realized.

2 You would set about undertaking an analysis of year 1 to anticipate future trends and inform suitable strategies for the achievement of the year 2 targets.

3 You would call a team meeting to present an analysis of year 1 and what you believe will be the future trends and best strategies to achieve the year 2 targets.

4 You would call a team meeting where you would review year 1 and present the targets for year 2 and assign to members of the team the task of predicting future trends and the brainstorming of strategies for the achievement of the year 2 targets.

| Your answer | 1 | 2 | 3 | 4 |

Situation 7

You noticed that two of your team members who had previously worked well together have, since a reorganization, started to blame each other for even the slightest problem and now bicker over responsibilities.

Rate the suggested responses as:

A. The most appropriate response
B. An acceptable response
C. A less than acceptable response

These are the suggested responses:

1 You would call a team meeting and re-communicate the roles assigned to each member of the team at the reorganization.

2 You would call a team meeting and explain that you have noticed that there seems some confusion over roles and responsibilities since the reorganization.

3 You would review the assignment of roles to see if there was any unintentional duplication or conflict and you would meet with the two individuals to discuss what you have noticed and seek their views on whether or not the assignment of roles can be adjusted to avoid doubling-up or clashes.

4 You would meet with the two individuals and re-communicate the roles assigned to them through the reorganization.

Your answer   1   2   3   4

Situation 8

Your partner organizations and stakeholders are very unhappy with the progress of the project you manage. You find out that they have called a meeting to discuss their next move but no one from your organization has been invited.

Rate the suggested responses as:

A. The most appropriate response
B. An acceptable response
C. A less than acceptable response

These are the suggested responses:

1 You would immediately set about calling as many of the partners and stakeholders as possible to discuss their dissatisfaction and what can be done to address it.

2 You would immediately inform your line manager of what you have discovered.

3 You would attend the meeting.

4 You would request that minutes are kept of the meeting and that these are shared with you.

Your answer   1   2   3   4

Situation 9

In your organization there are four levels of alert to notify managers of a problem. The lowest is a notice of concern where you notify managers that things are going less well than expected and need to be closely monitored. Yellow alert is the second level of alarm and is used to notify managers that a project is at risk of failure and requires remedial action in the short term. Orange alert is the second from highest level of alarm and is used to notify managers that prompt action is required if failure is to be averted. The highest level is a red alert, which signifies that a project is on the brink of failure and that extensive and urgent measures are required.

You are responsible for the delivery of a one-year flagship project and for the first two quarters the project has failed to achieve targets. When the project failed to realize output the first time you signalled a notice of concern. When the second quarter's results were published you raised the alarm to yellow alert. You now have the third quarter's results and are relieved that they are slightly better than quarter 2 but still well below the target.

Rate the suggested responses as:

A. The most appropriate response
B. An acceptable response
C. A less than acceptable response

These are the suggested responses:

1 You would lower the alert to a notice of concern.

2 You would leave the alert at yellow.

3 You would issue an orange alert.

4 You would issue a red alert.

Your answer   1   2   3   4

Situation 10

A colleague confided in you that another colleague was behaving in-appropriately towards her. The same day the colleague about whom she complained came to you and stated that he felt humiliated and embarrassed when at the team meeting you discussed in front of everyone the under-performance of the part of the project he was responsible for. He explained that in his view your concerns should have been raised in a one-to-one meet-ing and not in the team meeting. You agree that a one-to-one meeting is a good idea.

Rate the suggested responses as:

A. The most appropriate response
B. An acceptable response
C. A less than acceptable response

These are the suggested responses:

1 At the meeting you would tell him about the report of the inappropriate behaviour and explain that you expect it to stop immediately.

2 At the meeting you would start by telling him about the report of inappropriate behaviour and ask to hear his version of events, and then raise the issue of how you handled the underperformance of his part of the project at the team meeting.

3 You would start the meeting by discussing the issue of how you handled the underperformance of his part of the project at the team meeting and then tell him about the report of inappropriate behaviour and how you would like to hear his version of events.

4 At the meeting you would explain how it had not been your intention to humiliate or embarrass him at the team meeting. You would hear him out and then tell him of the report of inappropriate behaviour and ask him if he has anything to say on the matter.

Your answer   1   2   3   4

CHAPTER 3

Great candidate except for the maths!

Research indicates that one in six graduates lacks confidence in the use of percentages, averages and the interpretation of tabulated data.

These findings are hardly surprising, given that a lot of graduates leave higher education having not studied maths for many years. If this research describes you, then you need to revise forgotten rules and build up your confidence, speed and accuracy.

You may well require more material than is contained here and you can obtain more from the following titles in the Kogan Page Testing list:

The Numeracy Test Workbook
Ultimate Psychometric Tests, 2nd edition
How to Pass Data Interpretation Tests

If you are a business studies graduate or have completed a course of study that required you to be supernumerate, then you may be able to skip the early parts of this chapter. Before you do, you may want to work through the data interpretation test towards the end. If you face a test in which you are not allowed a calculator, you will find this chapter ideal for revision. You can obtain further advanced numerical questions in the following Kogan Page Testing titles:

How to Pass Advanced Numeracy Tests, 2nd edition
The Graduate Psychometric Test Workbook, 2nd edition
The Advanced Numeracy Test Workbook, 2nd edition

There are very few graduate recruitment schemes that do not include a psychometric test of your numerical skills. If you are applying to one of the major professional services firms, accountancy firms or banks, you can be sure that the process will include a challenging numerical test.

The company Ernst & Young currently requires you to sit two numerical tests! The first is online, and if you pass that, there follows a second, invigilated pen and paper test.

In many graduate numerical tests a calculator will be provided. However, if you are applying to a great many organizations, you should realize that a calculator is not always provided.

Deutsche Bank is currently using a numerical test in which a calculator is not allowed.

Even when a calculator is given, your mental arithmetic needs to be good enough for you to know when you have made a mistake.

So, practise lots and get your mental arithmetic back into shape. Remember, you may well have to complete a test without a calculator. For this reason, the practice material in this chapter has been designed to be completed without a calculator. You will find below, at the intermediate level:

1 A diagnostic exercise of key competencies to help you establish the extent to which you need to practise and the areas in which you need to practise most.

2 A glossary of key terms so that you can revise the key operations.

At the intermediate and advanced level you will find:

3 Practice questions and practice timed tests. These questions and tests get progressively harder and introduce the level of questions that you can expect to face in a real test.

At the advanced level:

4 The chapter concludes with a data interpretation test representative of the level of numerical test that you can expect in a graduate recruitment campaign for a financial role.

A key skills diagnostic exercise

The airline Cathay Pacific uses an online numeracy test that consists of 33 questions and is time limited to 30 minutes. It comprises five or six scenarios involving graphs, tables and figures. Each scenario has five or six questions. Each question has 16 possible answers to choose from. Using pencil and paper is allowed, but not a calculator. A favourite assignment involves the conversion of currencies.

No one seems to make it through the whole exam.

Allow yourself 30 minutes to attempt the following 33 questions. As for the Cathay Pacific test, attempt these questions without a calculator. Note that this diagnostic does not set scenarios and questions but instead examines your command of the competencies required for a winning score in the Cathay Pacific tests and others like it. Once you have completed this test, score it and then read the interpretation of your score that follows the test.

Try to complete the test without interruption and, remember, without a calculator.

Complete the following conversions between fractions, decimals and percentages. Express all fractions in their lowest form.

1 $3/4$ $= ?$ $= ?$ *Answer* [   ]

2 $? =$ 0.2 $= ?$ *Answer* [   ]

3 $? =$ $?$ $= 60\%$ *Answer* [   ]

4 $? =$ 0.375 $= ?$ *Answer* [   ]

5 $1/4$ $= ?$ $= ?$ *Answer* [   ]

Currency exchange:
1 USD = 88.25 JPY
1 EUR = 1.47 USD
1 GBP = 11.82 ZAR
1 AUD = 0.97 USD
1 RUB = 0.022 EUR

6   How many JPY are the equivalent to 40 USD?

Answer [   ]

7   What value in EUR are equivalent to 200 RUB?

Answer [   ]

8 Which suggested answer is the closest inverse exchange rate for GBP = ZAR?

A 1 ZAR: 0.0845 GBP

B 1 ZAR: 0.0846 GBP

C 1 ZAR: 0.0847 GBP

D 1 ZAR: 0.0848 GBP   *Answer* [   ]

9 If 1 GBP = 1.4 USD what is the inverse rate?

Answer [   ]

10 Parked in a street are 14 cars and four motorcycles. What is the ratio of cars to motorcycles?

Answer [   ]

11 A shop sold three watches at £16, a ring at £30 and four travelling alarm clocks at £9 each. What was the average sale price? (£1 = 100 pence)

Answer [   ]

12 A pair of shoes is normally priced at £37. What will be the sale price if a 25% discount is offered? (£1 = 100 pence)

Answer [   ]

13 A fuel mix comprises 14 parts fuel to 1 part oil. How much fuel will be present in 9 litres of mixed fuel? (1 litre = 100 centilitres)

Answer [   ]

14 If a local heath authority spent $6 million on distribution for the 15 million items of literature it sent out last year what is the average price for distribution per item? ($1 = 100 cents)

A 2.5 cents   B 4 cents   C 25 cents   D 40 cents

Answer [   ]

15   A railway wagon can be loaded with $20\frac{1}{8}$ metric tonnes of flour in $12\frac{1}{2}$ kg bags. How many bags of flour can the wagon hold? (1 metric tonne = 1,000 kg)

Answer _____

16   Every time a machine rotates it stamps one compact disc. A buyer agrees to buy each disc for 16 cents. If the machine runs for 30 minutes at 1,200 revolutions a minute what will be the total cost of the discs produced?

Answer _____

17   The period sales figures for your department are illustrated in the table against your targets. How many unit sales must you achieve in the last period if you are to achieve your target?

Period	Sales achieved	Targets
1	24	30
2	13	20
3	17	22
4	20	22
5	19	22
6		20

Answer _____

18   To pass an exam candidates had to average 60 marks across four papers. After three papers one candidate's score is averaging 52. What mark must the candidate achieve in the final paper to pass the four papers?

Answer _____

19 An invoice totals £5,000 and includes tax at 10%. Which is the nearest estimate of the cost of the services or goods excluding tax?

A £4,500

B £4,525

C £4,545

D £4,575   Answer [ ]

Complete the sequence:

20 2, 5, 8, 11, ?, 17   Answer [ ]

21 3, 4, 12, 48, ?   Answer [ ]

22 4, 9, 16, 25, ?   Answer [ ]

23 A shop buys a watch for £10 and sells it for £16. What is the percentage gross profit?

          Answer [ ]

24 A receiver has to share a sum of money between three creditors. Creditor X is to receive $1,000 more than creditor Y. Creditor Z is to receive three times as much as creditor Y. Identify the equation which allows you to establish that creditor X will receive $1,600 if creditor Z is paid £1,800.

A $X = 1600/3 + 1,000$

B $X = 1,800/3 + 1,000$

C $X = 1600 \times 3 - 1,000$

D $X = 1800 \times 3 - 1,000$ Answer [ ]

25 Match the number to its reciprocal.

A	25	B	20	C	10	D	8
1	0.04	2	0.1	3	0.125	4	0.05

          Answer [ ]

26 Which of the following are both squared and cubed numbers?

1, 8, 27, 64, 125, 216   *Answer* [   ]

27 How many whole number factors does 18 have (including 1 and 18)?

A 4   B 5   C 6   D 7   E 8

Answer [   ]

28 On a scale of 0–5 an independent reviewer rated a holiday at a disappointing 1.5. What is the percentage equivalent of this rating?

Answer [   ]

29 What is the percentage change between 45 and 48 minutes passed an hour?

Answer [   ]

30 Over a five-day period 600 people visited an attraction. 1/3 attended on day one and 5/12 attended on day two. How many attendees visited the attraction over the last three days?

Answer [   ]

31 If a company makes a total of 4,050 T-shirts in the colours red, blue and white in the ratio 1:3:5, how many blue T-shirts did the company produce?

Answer [   ]

32 If $3a + b = 6$ and $2a + 2b = 12$, then $2b - 2a$ is:

A 8   B 10   C 6   D 18   E 12

Answer [   ]

33　If 4a = 3b and 6b = 0 then:

　　A　3/4　　　　　　　　　B　a = b

　　C　a = 3 and b = 4　　　D　a/b = 4/3

　　E　b/a = 3/4

Answer

An interpretation of your score in the diagnostic exercise

A score of 27 or above

If you face one of the high-level numerical tests produced by SHL or PSL because you are applying for a graduate traineeship in a financial department in a leading international consultancy or banking, then this is the only score that you can be content with. To excel in these tests you must demonstrate a grasp of the fundamental operations in maths and answer questions such as these with confidence, accuracy and total familiarity.

Move on to the tests towards the end of this chapter and practise under realistic conditions.

You will find further advanced-level practice in the Kogan Page title *How to Pass Advanced Numeracy Tests*, 2nd edition.

A score of 20–27

Establish which of the key operations you got wrong and start a programme of practice that focuses most on these operations. You will find many suitable questions in this title but you will need more practice material than is contained in this volume. So, source lots more practice questions. You will find hundreds more in the following Kogan Page books:

The Graduate Psychometric Test Workbook, 2nd edition
Ultimate Psychometric Tests, 2nd edition

Keep practising until you have fully revised these essential operations. Be prepared to commit a quite considerable amount of time to your programme of revision. Once you feel that you have mastered the challenge then move on to take the practice tests towards the end of this chapter.

A score below 20

Don't attend an ability test of your numerical skills until you have completely revised the key mathematical operations in this book. This may require a quite considerable commitment in terms of time and effort. You will need many more questions than are contained in this book. You can find hundreds of suitable questions in the following Kogan Page titles:

The Numeracy Test Workbook
Ultimate Psychometric Tests, 2nd edition
How to Pass Data Interpretation Tests

Once you have completed these, you can move on to the more difficult material found in this chapter and the recommended titles for candidates who scored 20 or above. Don't give up; just keep practising. This is definitely something you can learn. It is only a matter of time and commitment.

Glossary of key terms and methods

If it is some years since you studied mathematics, then it is important that you remind yourself of the meanings of key terms and methods.

The following glossary of terms is intended only as a reminder. The suggested methods are by no means the only way to work the calculations. If you rely on another method, then it is probably best if you stick with it.

Make sure that you can operate quickly, accurately and with confidence the following rules and methods.

Addition

If the numbers have the same sign (positive or negative), then you add them together and use the same sign in the number. If the numbers have different signs, then apply the rule that $+ -$ is the same as $-$. For example:

$$2 + -6 = -4$$
$$16 + -2 = 14$$

If you subtract a smaller number from a larger one, the answer will be positive. If you subtract a large number from a smaller one, the result will be negative.

Angle

Angles are measured in degrees and record the amount of turn. A right angle has 90 degrees, an obtuse angle is greater than 90 but less than 180 degrees, and a reflex angle is greater than 180 degrees. Angles on a straight line add up to 180 degrees, while angles from a point add up to 360 degrees.

Area

Area is a two-dimensional measurement. To work out the area of a square, you multiply the length of one side by itself. All areas are measured in squares, eg square centimetres. To establish the area of a rectangle, multiply length by width. The area occupied by a triangle is established by multiplying its height by half the length of its base line.

Average

The average, or arithmetic *mean*, is found by adding up all the figures and dividing the total by the number of figures. *Average* differs from *mode*, which is the item of data that occurs the most often, and *median*, which is the figure or item of data that is in the middle once all the items have been put into a specific order.

Bar chart

A bar chart is a visual representation of data that allows the viewer to make comparisons between the frequency or quantity of items. It is used when the horizontal scale is simply a list. The bars are of equal width; the frequency or quantity is illustrated by the height of the bar.

Brackets

When there appear to be several ways in which to proceed with a calculation, to ensure that the calculation proceeds in the correct order, the items to be calculated first are enclosed within brackets. Work out the parts in brackets first. Brackets are sometimes referred to as a 'first priority'. A second priority is multiplication and division, which must be done before the third priority: addition and subtraction.

Circle

The circumference of a circle is the outer edge and is calculated with the equation pi × diameter. A *cord* is any straight line drawn from one part of the circumference to another. When a circle has a cord drawn on it, the circle is divided into two *segments*. A straight line taken from the circumference to the centre is called the *radius*; and a straight line taken from one part of the circumference to another, passing through the centre, is called the *diameter*. The area of a circle is equal to pi × the square of its radius.

Congruency

If shapes, for example squares or triangles, have the same angle and all the lengths are the same, they are said to be *congruent*. Shapes are said to be *similar* if the angles are the same and the ratios of all the corresponding lengths are equal.

Cube

A cube has six square faces at right angles to each other. The cube of a number is established if the number is multiplied by itself twice: for example, the cube of 5 = 5 × 5 × 5 (answer 125). The cube root of 125 is therefore 5. The sign for cube root 3 is $\sqrt[3]{}$.

Decimal number

A decimal number has a decimal point. The point serves to separate the whole number from the decimal fraction. Some decimals are recurring. Decimal places after the point represent, respectively, tenths, hundredths, thousandths, and so on.

Distance

To calculate distance, multiply rate of travel by time.

Division

It is unusual in a psychometric test to have to undertake long division, especially if the sum is awkward. Some test publishers, however, may want to establish whether you are aware of short cuts and patterns in mathematics. For this reason it is worth looking to see whether the question has been formed so as to test, for example, whether you realize one of the following:

- A number is divisible by 2 if the last digit is even.
- A number is divisible by 5 if its last digit is either 5 or 0 and by 10 if its last digit is 0 (to divide by 10, simply take off the 0).
- A number is divisible by 3 if the sum of its digits is divisible by 3.
- A number is divisible by 9 if the sum of its digits is divisible by 9.
- A number is divisible by 4 if the number formed by the last two digits is divisible by 4.
- A number is divisible by 8 if the number formed by the last three digits is divisible by 8.
- A number is divisible by 6 if it is also divisible by both 2 and 3.

Exponent

An exponent is the power to which something has been raised. For example, in the term 10 to the power of 2 the exponent is 2, and this is expressed as 10^2.

Factor

A factor is a whole number that will divide into another number exactly. The factors of, for example, 8 are 1, 2, 4 and 8.

Factorizing

If you factorize an equation or mathematical expression, you separate it into bracketed parts which, if multiplied together, will give that expression.

Fractions

A fraction is a part of a whole number. You need to be able to work with both decimal and vulgar fractions. Decimal fractions are described in the entry entitled 'decimal number'. Vulgar fractions use whole numbers one above the other; the lower number is called the denominator and the upper number is called the numerator. An improper fraction is one where the numerator is bigger than the denominator.

Fractions can be changed to another, equivalent fraction and still have the same value. You should always finish a calculation by expressing a fraction in its lowest term.

To change a fraction to a lower equivalent you look to divide both the numerator and denominator by the same number. This is called *cancelling*. If the number is even, you can always divide by 2. Sometimes you cancel more than once before you arrive at the lowest equivalent.

To add or subtract fractions you need to ensure that all the denominators are the same. In the example

$$\frac{1}{2} + \frac{3}{8} = ?$$

you find the common denominator, which is 8, and convert to eighths $= \frac{4}{8} + \frac{3}{8}$

The answer is $\frac{7}{8}$.

To multiply fractions, make sure that any mixed numbers (whole numbers and fractions) are converted into improper fractions and then multiply all the numerators and all the denominators together.

To divide fractions, change any mixed numbers into improper fractions and then turn the fraction by which you are dividing upside down (invert it) and multiply.

Frequency

Frequency is the number of times an event occurs.

Generalization

If we find a pattern and express it using algebraic expressions, we are said to have *generalized* it.

Graph

A graph is a diagram comprising two reference lines, called axes, at right angles to each other. A scale is marked along each axis. Graphs are used to show a relationship between two quantities. Before you begin to calculate with figures taken from a graph, take care to establish that the units are comparable and that you are looking in the correct column or line. See *x and y*.

Histogram

A histogram is similar to a bar chart except that it is the areas of the bars that represent the frequency or quantity rather than the length of the bars.

Inequalities

Inequalities are signs used to indicate relative size. Examples you must understand are:

> means 'greater than'
< means 'less than'.

Interest: compound and simple

You may well face questions that require you to work out simple or, more likely, compound interest.

Simple interest involves a quantity of money and a rate of interest. You simply multiply the amount of money by the rate of interest and divide by 100 to establish the interest earned.

Compound interest is the type most banks offer. The interest is added to the amount saved and you then receive interest on both the amount saved and the interest earned. The total compound interest can be roughly estimated by using the following formula, which if applied will save time. Try it and decide its value for yourself:

Final amount = P × (R/100)N + P

where P = amount initially invested (the *principal*), R = percentage rate of interest and N = number of years for which the investment is made.

Mean, median and mode

See *Average* (above).

Multiplication

Make sure the units of each number are underneath each other. To multiply any whole number by 10, 100, 1,000 and so on, simply add a 0 in the case of multiplying by 10, two 0s in the case of 100, etc.

To multiply decimals, ignore the decimal point and proceed as if the numbers were whole. When you have finished multiplying, count for each decimal how many figures (including 0s) there are to the right of the decimal point and add them together. The total gives you the number of decimal figures to the right of the point you must have in your answer.

Percentage

Percentage is a way of describing parts of a whole. One per cent (1%) represents one out of a hundred. To calculate, for example, 25% of 300 we calculate:

$$300 \times {}^{25}/_{100} = 75$$

Percentage as a fraction. A percentage is a fraction with a denominator of 100. To express a percentage as a fraction, all you need do is express it as its lowest term.

Percentage as a decimal. To change a percentage into a decimal, all you need do is divide it by 100. You can do this by moving the decimal point two places towards the left.

Changing fractions and decimals into percentages. Multiply by 100.

Percentage decrease and increase. To work out a percentage decrease or increase, you compare the decrease or increase with the original amount.

If the amount is to be decreased by, for example, 20%, then we need to calculate 100 − 20 = 80% of the total. Likewise, if we want to increase an amount by, say, 10%, we have to calculate 10% of the original amount.

To work out 80% of £14 we use the following method:

$$(80/100) \times 14 = £11.20$$

Value added tax and profit and loss

Test questions of percentage are often concerned with value added tax (VAT) or profit and loss.

VAT

Ensure that you are able to work out the amount of VAT to be charged and the amount of VAT contained in an inclusive sum. The first of these is easy. To work out the VAT contained in a total, use the following method:

Treat the inclusive sum as 100% + the percentage rate of VAT. Then work out 100% of the total.

For example, how much VAT (charged at 17.5%) is contained in an inclusive sum of £47? To answer this, take 47 = 117.5%. Now find 100%: 1% = 47/117.5 = 0.4, so 100% = 40. So the VAT is £47 – £40 = £7.

You can also find VAT by multiplying the total, inclusive of VAT at 17.5%, by 7.47.

Profit and loss

We buy goods at one price and sell them at another. Test questions often expect profit and loss to be expressed as a percentage. The way to approach these questions is as follows:

1 Work out the cash profit or loss.

2 Express this as a fraction of the original (buying) price.

3 Convert this fraction to a percentage.

Pi

The sign for pi is π and is found by dividing the circumference of a circle by its diameter.

Pictogram

A pictogram is a representation of information which uses pictures to denote the frequency or quantity.

Pie chart

A pie chart divides a circle into sectors the size of which represents a portion of the whole.

Powers

See *Exponent*.

Priorities

See *Brackets*.

Probability

The likelihood of an event happening can be expressed. The comparison can be shown as, for example, a fraction, percentage or ratio (see below). If something is considered impossible, then the probability is 0; if there is an even chance of its happening, it is expressed as $\frac{1}{2}$; and if an event is a certainty it is expressed as 1. The probability of a dice being rolled and its coming to rest with the number 3 at the top is 1/6.

Quartiles

If you have a graph demonstrating the cumulative frequency of a quantity, it may be divided into equal quarters, and these are called quartiles of a distribution. Quartiles are added to the graph by dividing the total frequency into equal groups. You have an upper and lower quartile and the median.

Ratio

Ratio is a comparison of quantities. Like fractions, they can be simplified or cancelled down. For example, if you are told that the ratio of men to women is 25:50, this can be simplified to 1:2.

Running totals or cumulative frequency

A running total allows you to realize the total to date and find out the median and the quartiles of distribution. If drawn on a graph, the cumulative frequency will form a distinctive curve known as the *ogive*.

Sequence tests

For many candidates, sequencing tests offer the chance to show considerable improvement through practice. They really are a lot easier than they at first seem.

A sequence is offered with one of the set missing, which you have to identify. The sequence can start and end at any point. The most common types are as follows:

Addition

The sequence for adding the number 8 can be presented as:

480, 488, 496, 504, 512, 520, 528, and so on.

Subtraction

If a sequence is decreasing from left to right, it may be the result of subtraction. Subtraction of the number 6 can be illustrated as follows:

540, 534, 528, 522, 516, 510, 504 ...

Multiplication

This common type of sequence is constructed as a result of multiplying the same number each time. The sequence derived by the multiplication of 3 is, for example, as follows:

2, 6, 18, 54, 162, 486 ...

Division

In a way similar to multiplication, a sequence can be constructed as a result of division. For example, division by 5 each time produces the following sequence:

37,500, 7,500, 1,500, 300, 60 ...

Add two previous terms

This type of sequence is generated by adding the two previous numbers to obtain the next in the series. For example:

1, 4, 5, 9, 14, 23, 37 ...

Multiply two previous numbers

Related to the previous example, this sequence is obtained by multiplying the two previous digits:

3, 4, 12, 48, 576 ...

Alternating signs

A number may have either a positive or a negative sign, and the sign of the numbers that make up a sequence may be alternated in an attempt to make it less recognizable. For example:

2, –4, 8, –16, 32, –64, 128 ...

Addition of two common sequences

Take the sequence:

1, 2, 4, 7, 11, 16, 22, 29, 37, 46 ...

It is produced by adding a term from the sequence 1, 2, 3, 4, 5, 6, 7, 8, 9 to the previous number. To get 2 we add 1 to the first term, to get 4 we add 2 to 2, to get 7 we add 3 to 4, and so on. This type of sequence is produced as a result of adding a number to the first term to get the second but adding a different number to get the fourth. You work out what number to add each time because these numbers belong to another sequence.

Hidden series

Sometimes the test author will try to hide a sequence by presenting it in a misleading manner. For example:

123, 456, 789, 101, 112, 131, 415, 161, 718 ...

All the test author has done in this instance is present the most common sequence of all in a different way. The sequence is the numbers 1–18.

Sequences worth remembering

The following sequences come up often and are worth committing to memory if they are not familiar:

The power of 2 sequence 2, 4, 8, 16, 32, 64, 128, 256 ...
The power of 3 sequence 3, 9, 27, 81, 243, 729 ...
The square of numbers 1, 4, 9, 16, 25, 36, 49, 64, 81, 100 ...
A sequence of factors 1, 2, 6, 24, 120, 720 ...
The cubes of numbers 1, 8, 27, 64, 125, 216 ...

The power of 4 sequence 4, 16, 64, 256, 1024 ...
The sequence of prime numbers 1, 2, 3, 5, 7, 11, 13, 17, 19, 23, 29 ...

Set

A set is a collection or class of items that have something in common. In mathematics a set is indicated by this type of bracket { }. An example of a set (in this case a finite set) is the set of positive numbers to 10: {1 2 3 4 5 6 7 8 9 10}.

Square root

The square root of a number is that number which, if multiplied by itself, would give your original number. For example, the square root of 25 is 5 because $5 \times 5 = 25$. Every number has both a positive and a negative square root. The square roots of 25 are both 5 and –5 (remember, if two negative numbers are multiplied, they equal a positive number).

Subtraction

There are two widely practised methods of subtraction. I will illustrate them with the following example:

$$
\begin{array}{r}
93 \\
- 27 \\
\hline
66
\end{array}
$$

In method A, you would borrow 10 from the 9 to make the $3 = 13$; the 9 would then become an 8. In method B, we would again add 10 to the 3 to make it 13 but this time we would also add 10 to the 2 on the bottom line to make it 3.

Stick with whichever method you were taught and practise to make sure you are accurate and quick.

Triangle

The sum of the inside angles of a triangle is always 180 degrees. An equilateral triangle is one with three equal sides and three equal angles, all 60 degrees. A right-angled triangle is one with a right angle. An isosceles triangle is one with two equal sides and two equal angles.

Volume

Volume is the measurement of the three-dimensional space occupied by a solid. It is quantifiable in cubic measurement, for example cubic metres.

There are formulae for finding volume in all the regular shapes. To find the volume of a box, for instance, you multiply length by breadth by height. To find the volume of shapes that have vertical sides of equal lengths, for example a cylinder or a triangular prism, you multiply the area of the base by the height.

Whole numbers

Examples of whole numbers are 0, 1, 2, 3, 4, and so on. A whole number that is divisible by 2 is called an even number. A number not divisible by 2 is an odd number. Note that a number is said to be divisible only if a second number divides into it without any remainder.

x and y

The horizontal (x) and vertical (y) axes on a two-dimensional graph are referred to as the x and y axes.

Sixty practice number problems

This style of question has been around for decades and still remains a firm favourite. If the test you face comprises this style of question, then make sure that you keep practising until you are really quick and get the vast majority of these questions right. Even if you do not face number problems, use this style of question to revise your command of mathematical operations.

1 A till roll is 10 metres long while the average till receipt is 8 centimetres long. How many customers can be served before the till roll needs to be changed?

Answer [   ]

2 A store serves 6,000 customers a day. Given that the average till receipt is 8 centimetres long and a till roll is 10 metres long, how many till rolls will be used each day?

Answer [   ]

3 A household's water bill is £240 and is charged at 15 pence a gallon. How many gallons of water does the household use?

Answer [   ]

4 A household's water bill of £240 is to increase by 12%. What will be the new total?

Answer [   ]

5 If a water bill of $240 includes VAT at 17.5%, how much VAT will be paid? Express your answer to the nearest whole cent.

Answer [   ]

6 The pages of a novel have on average 50 lines comprising 12 words. If in total there are 175 pages, how many words does the novel contain?

Answer [   ]

7 A cyclist averages 7.5 miles an hour on level ground but only 4.5 miles an hour going uphill. If the ratio between flat ground and hills is 1:3, what is the cyclist's average speed in mph over 60 miles?

Answer [   ]

8 A publisher must sell 20,000 books at an average unit cost of £7.60 to break even. If salaries account for 40% of expenditure, how much is the wages bill?

Answer

9 A box of chocolates comprises 12 chocolates and weighs three-quarters of a kilogram. If the packaging weighs ⅕ of the total, how much does each chocolate weigh? Express your answer as a fraction of a kilogram.

Answer

10 A garage discovered that ½ of its customers bought French cars, ⅓ German cars and ⅙ (20) American cars. How many customers did the garage have?

Answer

11 How much is three-fifths of $750?   *Answer*

12 One-half of the turnover of a business is spent on salaries, one-third on production and distribution. After setting aside £10,000 for marketing, there is £23,000 left. How much is the total turnover?

Answer

13 In a sale, goods were advertised at one-quarter of their marked price. What was the total sales price for:

a calculator, marked price $5.90?

a book, marked price $17.30?

jeans, marked price $44.00?   *Answer*

14 To travel to work, a woman spends 70 cents on a bus fare and 120 cents on a train fare. She spends the same amount on the way home. In a normal working week, how much would she save if she bought a travel pass at $14.50?

Answer

15   A man purchased a lottery ticket each week (52 weeks a year) for six years. He worked out that he would have to win £624 to recoup his money. How much did each ticket cost?

Answer

16   A full-price ticket to Liverpool costs £84. If you travel after 9.30 am the cost drops to £32. What percentage saving does this represent?

Answer

17   There are only 24 women out of a total workforce of 1,200 in an engineering company. What is the ratio of female to male employees?

Answer

18   From an initial fee of £600 a company had to credit back to the customer £96 to cover a dry-cleaning bill. What is the percentage refund?

Answer

19   Find the compound interest on $2,000 invested for 3 years at 5% per annum (pa).

Answer

20   A 16-kilogram sack of potatoes costs £4.50. How much does a kilogram of potatoes cost? Express your answer to the nearest whole penny.

Answer

21   A bank offers 6% pa interest calculated annually. Another offers 10% pa compound interest calculated every six months. What is the difference paid at the end of the year on a deposit of $1,000?

Answer

22 A new ship is 300 feet long and its plans are on a scale of 1:200. How long is the ship as it is represented on the plans?

Answer [　　　　　]

23 An investment of £10,000 earns interest at 6% pa fixed for a 5-year period. How much will the total investment with interest amount to at the end of the 5-year period?

Answer [　　　　　]

24 A business loan of $2,000 is to have interest charged at 20% pa. How much will the monthly repayments be if both the interest and the loan are to be repaid in one year?

Answer [　　　　　]

25 The interest on a car loan of £3,000 is to be charged at 15% pa. How much will the monthly repayments be if both the loan and interest are to be repaid in 24 months? Express your answer to the nearest penny.

Answer [　　　　　]

26 A box of 100 pens is bought for £5 and the pens are sold for 8 pence each. What is the percentage profit?

Answer [　　　　　]

27 A table was sold for $280 at a 20% loss. What was the buying price?

Answer [　　　　　]

28 A watch costs £9.00 plus VAT, which is charged at 17.5%. What is the total price to be paid?

Answer [　　　　　]

29 An estimate is made for $2,000 plus tax (at 17.5%) for the preparation of a business plan. How much tax is to be paid?

Answer [　　　　　]

30   A restaurant bill totals £110.00 inclusive of VAT and a service charge. VAT was charged at 17.5% after a service charge of 10% had been levied. How much was the bill excluding the VAT and service charge? Express your answer to the nearest penny.

Answer [   ]

31   A photocopier service contract costs $40 a month excluding tax (at 17.5%). How much tax is paid in 12 months?

Answer [   ]

32   A cooker is sold for £800 inclusive of VAT, which is charged at 17.5%. How much did the cooker cost excluding VAT?

Answer [   ]

33   Divide $50 into the ratio of 3:2.   *Answer* [   ]

34   Components A, B and C are ordered in the ratio 1:5:4. How many of each is included in an order that totals 1,000 components?

Answer [   ]

35   In some areas in the United Kingdom, male unemployment is as high as 30% of the total economically active population. Express this level of unemployment as a ratio.

Answer [   ]

36   On a housing estate, 60% of the unemployed were found to have last worked in the construction industry, while 24% last worked in the public service sector and 16% last worked in retail and distribution. Express these quantities as a ratio.

Answer [   ]

37 The ratio of unemployed graduates to unemployed people without any kind of qualification is 1:8. If 30 unemployed graduates are found to use a resource centre, how many unemployed people with no qualification might be expected to attend?

Answer

38 A woman earns £13,000 and has a tax-free single person's allowance of £2,800. How much tax would she pay on her taxable earnings (assume the rate of tax is 24%).

Answer

39 A man earns £200 a week. He pays tax at 24% on all his earnings over his annual tax-free allowance of £2,300. How much tax does he pay each week? Express your answer to the nearest penny.

Answer

40 If tax is charged at 24%, how much is payable on a taxable income of £10,000?

Answer

41 A car travels 70 miles in $2\frac{1}{2}$ hours. What is its average speed?

Answer

42 A train travels at an average speed of 110 mph. How long does it take to travel 385 miles?

Answer

43 A yacht averages 4 nautical miles an hour but the tide is running against it at 1 knot. How long will the yacht take to reach a harbour 1.5 nautical miles away? (Note that 1 knot = 1 nautical mile an hour.)

Answer

44   The initial price on an item was £99 but it was reduced in a sale by 10%. After a week a further 10% discount was made on the new price. What was the eventual asking price?

Answer [   ]

45   A machine produces 130 nuts in 10 minutes. A second machine produces 264 nuts in 12 minutes. How long would it take the two machines running simultaneously to produce 700 nuts?

Answer [   ]

46   A total of 5,000 copies of a book were sold: 60% were sold at 50% discount, 20% were sold at 30% discount, while the remainder were sold at the cover price of £6.99. What was the total revenue?

Answer [   ]

47   In an election the Yellow Party candidate received half as many votes as the Red Party candidate. The Red Party candidate received one-third more votes than the candidate from the Blue Party. In total, 10,000 people voted for the Blue Party candidate. How many votes did the Yellow Party candidate receive?

Answer [   ]

48   In a sample of 220, 5% were positive. In a second sample of 120, 10% were positive. What was the combined number of positive responses?

Answer [   ]

49   A printer prints 20 characters a second and is 4 times as fast as the average printer. If the average printer is 5 times as fast as Jill, the copy typist, how many characters a second can Jill type?

Answer [   ]

50 After paying 24 per cent tax on all income over $2,300, a person has a net income of $12,000. What was the income before tax?

Answer [   ]

Find the missing numbers in the following sequences:

51 2, 5, 8, 11, ?, 17, 20   *Answer* [   ]

52 504, 512, 520, ?, 536   *Answer* [   ]

53 540, 534, 528, 522, 516, 510, ?   *Answer* [   ]

54 ?, 6, 18, 54, 162, 486   *Answer* [   ]

55 37,500, 7,500, ?, 300, 60   *Answer* [   ]

56 1, 4, ?, 9, 14, 23, 37   *Answer* [   ]

57 2, –4, 8, –16, 32, –64, ?   *Answer* [   ]

58 123, 456, 789, 101, 112, ?   *Answer* [   ]

59 3, 9, 27, 81, ?, 729   *Answer* [   ]

60 1, 8, 27, 64, 125, ?   *Answer* [   ]

End of test

Five practice tests

The remainder of this chapter is taken up with five realistic full-length practice tests. To get the most out of them, sit them as if they were real and stick to the time limits. To make the tests more realistic, set yourself the challenge of trying to beat your last score. Don't be too hard on yourself if you find this almost impossible, because the level of difficulty of the tests gets progressively harder. You will almost certainly be getting better as you practise even if you do not get a higher score each time, because the goalposts are moving.

These timed tests are intended only as practice timed tests and to serve primarily as an aid to learning, so do not read too much into the results. They should form a valuable part of your programme of self-study and they will help you develop an effective exam technique under realistic conditions and help you further to identify your strengths and address any weaknesses.

I have started with tests for the one in six graduates who lack confidence in the use of percentages, averages and the interpretation of tabulated data, and conclude with tests at the advanced level. The latter tests include a good number of questions at the level you might expect to get right if you were to obtain a good score in a real graduate test. What I mean by good is a score in the top 25 per cent of candidates. Setting the level of these timed tests is not a fine science, and while they may be appropriate for one candidate, I will not have got it right for others. You will find some hard questions to help you get used to the idea that you will not get them all right and should not spend too long on any one question.

Remember the most important thing: you have to try really hard to do well in a psychometric test.

Numerical test 1: Practice intermediate-level number problem test

The test that begins over the page comprises 30 numerical tasks for which you are allowed 25 minutes.

The questions are either multiple choice or short answer. You are required to work out the answer or identify which of the suggested answers is correct and enter the corresponding letter or answer in the answer box.

Do not use a calculator or other mechanical aid.

Do look at the suggested answers to see whether you can save time by estimating the answers.

When it helps, round sums up or down to more convenient amounts. If you cannot work out a question, practise educated guessing.

Make a note of the time and then turn the page and begin the mock test.

1   The plane is due to depart at 14.15 hours. You are required to check in one-and-a-half hours before departure and need to allow two hours to travel to the airport. What time would you need to leave home?

A	B	C	D	E	F
11.5	9.45	10.45	Noon	11.45	10.15

Answer

2   In 1995, 60 per cent of graduates were found to be poor at the interpretation of information when it was presented numerically. If there were 2,200 graduates that year, how many were able to interpret this kind of information?

A	B	C	D	E	F
1,320	1,100	2,200	1,400	880	1,000

Answer

3   A factory worker worked 37.5 hours a week. How many hours did she work over a 12-week period?

A	B	C	D	E	F
450	300	440	296	375	950

Answer

4   An office worker was required to keep a time sheet detailing how long it took to undertake each task. Excluding lunch, what was the total time taken to complete all the following tasks?

Franking mail	20 minutes
Amending computer files	45 minutes
Answering the telephone	70 minutes
Lunch	30 minutes

A	B	C	D	E	F
$2\frac{1}{2}$ hours	2 hours 5 minutes	2 hours	$1\frac{3}{4}$ hours	$2\frac{1}{4}$ hours	$1\frac{1}{2}$ hours

Answer

5 A survey in a café found that a quarter of all customers took sugar and an eighth took sweetener. What fraction of customers took no sugar or sweetener?

A	B	C	D	E	F
$3/5$	$9/16$	$3/8$	$5/8$	$1/2$	$1/20$

Answer [   ]

6 A survey found that $3/16$ths of women said that they would always shop at a complex that offered baby changing facilities; $5/8$ths said that they thought it advantageous if a complex offered this service; and the remaining 75 respondents indicated that they thought it made no difference. What number of women said they thought the service advantageous?

A	B	C	D	E	F
25	250	150	50	125	175

Answer [   ]

7 If a machine is designed to rotate 300 times a minute, how many rotations does it perform in an hour?

A	B	C	D	E	F
18 million	9,000	9 million	180,000	18,000	90,000

Answer [   ]

8 If the fastest student in the class can type at 30 words a minute, while the slowest can only manage 20 words, what would be the time difference between them if they undertook to input a document comprising 3,000 words?

A	B	C	D	E	F
50 minutes	1 hour	45 minutes	$1\frac{1}{4}$ hours	90 minutes	100 minutes

Answer [   ]

9 An architect designed a long, sweeping staircase which was a total of 16 metres in length. He specified that the staircase was to have 48 steps. Approximately, what was the length of each step?

A	B	C	D	E	F
$\frac{1}{2}$ metre	200 cm	$\frac{1}{4}$ metre	300 cm	400 cm	$\frac{1}{3}$ metre

Answer [   ]

10 It was recommended that the photocopier was serviced every half a million copies and on average it was used to undertake 70,000 copies a month. How many months should pass between services?

A	B	C	D	E	F
3	8	6	7	9	4

Answer [   ]

11 The head teacher of a school realized that he had overspent on the wages by 5 per cent. If the monthly total was supposed to be kept under $21,000, how much had been overspent?

A	B	C	D	E	F
$1,500	$950	$1,050	$1,175	$1,000	$700

Answer [   ]

12 A ship's engine was found to achieve a speed of 9 knots at 2,700 revolutions. How many extra revolutions would you expect to be required if the captain asked to increase the speed to 9.5 knots?

A	B	C	D	E	F
600	400	300	150	450	200

Answer [   ]

13 To build a product you use 16 parts costing 25 cents each and 42 parts at 19 cents each. What is the total build cost?

A	B	C	D	E	F
$13.73	$11.98	$13.29	$11.60	$13.54	$11.73

Answer [   ]

14 Your office referred 22 files to storage over a three-month period and they took up just over 4 metres of shelving. At that rate, how long would you expect it to take before your stored files occupied a kilometre of shelf space? (Answers are expressed in whole years.)

A	B	C	D	E	F
12 years	10 years	62 years	90 years	83 years	50 years

Answer [   ]

15 From what time should you book the conference room if the delegates' train arrives at 13.00 hours, the station is approximately 15 minutes away and you expect them to lunch with the Minister for two hours before the seminar begins?

A	B	C	D	E	F
Noon	4.00 pm	1.30 pm	3.15 pm	2.00 pm	2.45 pm

Answer [   ]

16 The photocopier operates at 45 copies a minute. How many minutes will it take to duplicate 1,100 copies?

A	B	C	D	E	F
20	50	21	55	24	19

Answer [   ]

17 Three departments decided to share equally the cost of a new piece of equipment. The bill totalled $3,780. How much did each department have to contribute?

A	B	C	D	E	F
$1,260	$260	$2,260	$1,890	$2,890	$890

Answer [   ]

18 A metre of rope cost 29 cents. How much would 120 metres cost?

A	B	C	D	E	F
$29.29	$36.50	$34.80	$37.10	$29.10	$29.00

Answer [   ]

19 If 350 people entered a competition and each paid $1.20, how much would remain if the organizer had to spend a total of $200 on prizes?

A	B	C	D	E	F
$220.20	$220	$22.40	$218.80	$217.60	$215.20

Answer [   ]

20 A pack of 8 sample pots of paint costs $7.68. What is the cost of each pot?

A	B	C	D	E	F
130 cents	85 cents	76.3 cents	109 cents	18 cents	96 cents

Answer [   ]

21 Most telephone calls were received between 10.00 and 11.00 am, which is three times as many as the 150 calls received between 3.00 and 4.00 pm. On average, how many calls a minute were received during the busiest hour?

A	B	C	D	E	F
6	150	$7\frac{1}{2}$	$2\frac{1}{2}$	16	450

Answer [   ]

22 A 50-gram item costs 25 pence to post. At the same rate, how much would you expect to pay to post an item that weighed a kilo?

A	B	C	D	E	F
£15	£150	£200	£500	£20	£5

Answer [   ]

23 If tax on a £150 television set is £22.50, how much tax is paid on a television that costs £1,050?

A	B	C	D	E	F
£157.50	£210.00	£183.75	£105.00	£73.50	£52.50

Answer [   ]

24   If it takes one person 5 hours to load a truck, while another person can complete the task in 3 hours, how long should it take them to half-fill the truck if they work together at the same rate?

A	B	C	D	E	F
2 hours	3 hours	4 hours	5 hours	6 hours	8 hours

Answer [   ]

25   One number is 3 times another and their sum is 28. What are the two numbers?

Answer [   ]

26   If 18% of the fuel is used, how many gallons did we start with if 492 gallons remains?

Answer [   ]

27   What is the sum of all the numbers from 18 through to 40?

Answer [   ]

28   Find three consecutive numbers that have the sum of 117.

Answer [   ]

29   If you cycle 6 times faster than you walk and you take in total 28 minutes to both cycle to work and walk the same distance back, how long did you spend walking?

A	B	C	D	E	F
28 minutes	26 minutes	24 minutes	14 minutes	4 minutes	2 minutes

Answer [   ]

30   How many numbers are there from 67 through to 99?

A	B	C	D	E	F
31	32	33	34	35	36

Answer [   ]

End of test

Numerical test 2: Practice intermediate-level sequencing test

Over the page you will find 26 practice sequencing questions. In each sequence two digits have been replaced with Xs. Alongside each question is a box where you must mark your answer.

Always enter two digits in your answer. If the answer is a single figure, enter a zero in front of it (eg 05).

Allow yourself 20 minutes to complete the test.

1   20   33   46   XX   72

Answer _____

2   6   9   XX   15   18

Answer _____

3   61   122   183   2XX   305

Answer _____

4   1,027963   8XX   835

Answer _____

5   5   10   20   XX   80

Answer _____

6   3   12   48   1XX   768

Answer _____

7   2   6   18   54   1XX

Answer _____

8   3   5   7   XX   11   13

Answer _____

9   64   32   16   XX   4   2   1

Answer _____

10   4   6   8   XX   12   14   16

Answer _____

11   20   18   16   14   XX   14   16   18   20

Answer _____

12   2   3   5   6   XX   9   11   12   14

Answer _____

13   5   7   10   14   XX   25   32   40

Answer [ ]

14   23   20   17   XX   11   8   5   Answer [ ]

15   ½   ¼   ¾   1   ⁷⁄₄   ˣˣ⁄₄   Answer [ ]

16   121   36   157   193   3XX   Answer [ ]

17   100   1   101   102   XX3   Answer [ ]

18   5   2   10   20   200   XX00   Answer [ ]

19   12   −24   36   −48   XX   Answer [ ]

20   42   −33   24   −15   XX   Answer [ ]

21   12   XX   −8   −6   4   2   Answer [ ]

22   2   −¼   6   −⅛   XX

Answer [ ]

23   1   3   7   15   XX

Answer [ ]

24   1   1⅓   9   ¹⁄₂₇   XX

Answer [ ]

25   4   10   28   82   XX4   730

Answer [ ]

26   11   12   113   124   33X   X46

Answer [ ]

End of test

Numerical test 3: Intermediate data interpretation practice test

Data interpretation tests seek to measure a candidate's ability to evaluate information and identify logical connections. You are provided with a passage describing a situation and a problem.

There are in total 30 questions in this test and you are allowed 25 minutes in which to complete them.

Note that the last 10 questions are of a different style from the first 20 questions. All the questions require you to read a situation or passage and answer questions, but the last 10 questions also require you to consider a list of additional information that may or may not resolve the problem. It is your task to identify from the list of five the item or items that solve the problem.

Unless you are required to, do not waste time working out the answers when you can identify the item or items of information required in order to establish the answer.

Do not use a calculator.

Situation 1

A factory is to commission two production lines. Production line 1 is to use the existing technology. Production line 2 is to use the latest innovations in technology, but while promising to achieve considerable advances in productivity, it will take longer to install and is likely to experience teething problems. Figure 1 illustrates the productive record of each production line. Refer to this graph in order to answer the following questions.

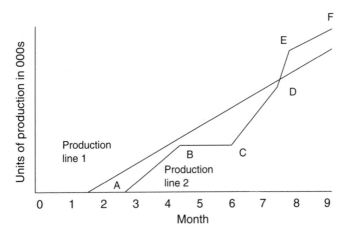

FIGURE 1

Question 1

In which month did production line 2 overtake production line 1 in the total number of units produced?

Answer [ ]

Question 2

From the information given, is it possible to attribute a reason why production line 1's record forms a straight line while production line 2's record takes the form of a polygon?

A   Yes, it is possible to attribute a reason

B   No, it is not possible to attribute a reason

C   You cannot tell whether it is possible or not

Answer [ ]

Question 3

The manager of production line 2 reported a complete breakdown. At what point did this occur?

A   Month 3

B   During month 4

C   Before month 4

D   You cannot tell   *Answer*

Question 4

Consider the following questions (A and B) and indicate whether both, either or neither can be answered, given the available data.

A   Can the duration of the reported breakdown be established?

B   Can the loss of production be quantified?

1. Both questions A and B can be answered
2. Only question A can be answered
3. Only question B can be answered
4. Neither question can be answered

Answer

Situation 2

Fifty candidates sat a test and the number of candidates who scored more than a specific number of correct answers is illustrated in Figure 2. Refer to this graph in order to answer the following questions.

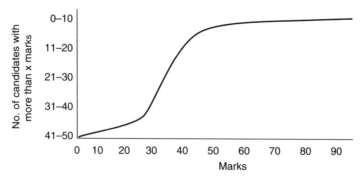

FIGURE 2

Question 5
What proportion of the candidates achieved over 50 correct marks?

A   The majority

B   A sizeable minority

C   Only a few

D   You cannot tell   *Answer*

Question 6
Is it possible to work out the median?

A   Yes, it is possible

B   No, it is not possible

C   You cannot tell whether it is possible or not

Answer

Question 7
A curve such as the one in Figure 2 is called a:

A   Polygon

B   Ogive

C   Parallel

D   None of these   *Answer*

Question 8
Consider the following questions (A and B) and indicate whether both, either or neither can be answered, given the available data.

A   Did the 50 candidates do well or badly in the test?

B   How many candidates got more than 70 marks out of 100?

1.   Both questions A and B can be answered

2.   Only question A can be answered

3.   Only question B can be answered

4.   Neither question can be answered

Answer

Situation 3

Women 16%   Women 18%   Women 20%

Area 1   Area 2   Area 3

FIGURE 3

The three pie charts shown in Figure 3 demonstrate the level of unemployment among women as a percentage of the economically active population
in three areas. The economically active population excludes people too old or
too young to work. The total economically active population for the three
areas is 55,000.

Question 9

Is it possible to work out the percentage level of unemployment for the total
populations of all three areas?

A   Yes, it is possible.

B   No, it is not possible.

C   You cannot tell whether it is possible or not.

Answer [   ]

Question 10

What is the mean percentage rate of unemployment for economically
active women across the three areas (assuming that the areas have equal
populations)?

A   18%   B   54%   C   3%   D   You cannot tell

Answer [   ]

Question 11

How many unemployed women are there?

A   22,500

B   More than half the total

C   Less than half the total

D   You cannot tell

Answer

Question 12

Consider the following questions (A and B) and indicate whether both, either or neither can be answered, given the available data.

A   Why are there more unemployed men than women?

B   What is the total working population across the three areas?

1.   Both questions A and B can be answered

2.   Only question A can be answered

3.   Only question B can be answered

4.   Neither question can be answered

Answer

Situation 4

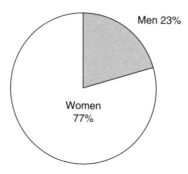

FIGURE 4a   The gender of customers who requested childcare facilities at the shopping arcade

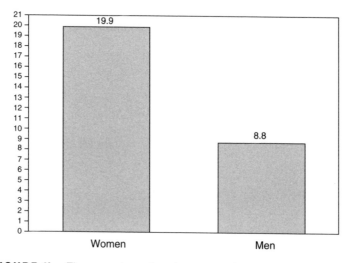

FIGURE 4b   The percentage of customers wanting childcare facilities who were willing to pay for the service

The managers of a shopping arcade undertook a process of customer consultation and found that high on the list of facilities requested by customers was a shoppers' crèche. In total, 800 customers took part in the survey, which was conducted during working hours between Monday 14 and Wednesday 16 May.

Question 13

What percentage of women who requested childcare facilities were also willing to pay to use the service?

A   19.9%   B   23%   C   77%   D   You cannot tell

Answer [   ]

Question 14

What percentage of male customers requested childcare facilities?

A   77%   B   8.8%   C   23%   D   You cannot tell

Answer [   ]

Question 15

Is it true to say that 100 per cent of customers who took part in the survey wanted childcare facilities at the arcade?

A   Yes   B   No   C   You cannot tell

Answer [   ]

Question 16

Consider the following questions (A and B) and indicate whether both, either or neither can be answered, given the available data.

A   What is the ratio of men to women customers who wanted childcare facilities?

B   How might the result have been affected had the management arranged for the survey to be carried out over the weekend rather than during the working week?

1.   Both questions A and B can be answered
2.   Only question A can be answered
3.   Only question B can be answered
4.   Neither question can be answered

Answer [   ]

Situation 5

The programmes director of a local radio station received the cohort shown in Figure 5, which compares the age and gender of listeners. During the period to which the cohort refers, 52 per cent of the station's audience were women. Most mornings, 125,000 families tune in for the breakfast show.

Use this information and the data contained in the cohort to answer the questions that follow.

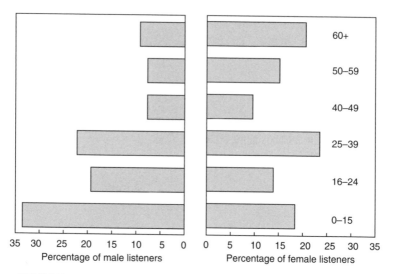

FIGURE 5   Age/gender cohort of local radio station listeners

Question 17

What percentage of male listeners are aged 15 years or under?

A   0–15%

B   Between 15 and 20%

C   Between 30 and 35%

D   You cannot tell

Answer [   ]

Question 18

What percentage of women aged between 16 and 24 years tune in to the station?

A   Just under 15%

B   20%

C   100%

D   You cannot tell

Answer

Question 19

What percentage of women listeners are aged 45 years?

A   Just over 10%

B   Just under 10%

C   You cannot tell

Answer

Question 20

Consider the following questions and indicate whether both, either or neither can be answered, given the available data.

A   What percentage of listeners are aged between 25 and 39 years?

B   With which age group is the station most popular?

1.   Both questions A and B can be answered

2.   Only question A can be answered

3.   Only question B can be answered

4.   Neither question can be answered

Answer

Question type 2

After reading the passage you must select from the suggested answers the additional piece or additional pieces of information that resolve the problem. It is your task to identify the item or items that solve the problem.

Question 21

A house plant and a decorative pot together retail at the inclusive price £3.75. Which two pieces of information do you require to establish the price of the pot before tax?

A The pot costs twice as much as a non-decorative equivalent.

B The pot costs three times as much as the plant, which is tax exempt.

C VAT in the United Kingdom is currently 17.5 per cent.

D An inclusive total is established by multiplying the exclusive price by the percentage rate of tax and adding this figure to the total.

E The price of an item excluding tax can be worked out from the inclusive total by multiplying by 0.036 and subtracting the answer from the total.

Answer [   ]

Question 22

A group of friends charter a yacht for their annual holiday. Which three pieces of information are necessary to establish the amount that they each had to contribute towards the deposit?

A Because it was the start of the season the trip cost £100; prices increased sixfold by July.

B The boat could sleep a maximum of six but one berth was spare.

C The holiday was to last two weeks.

D A 10 per cent deposit was payable with the booking and is refundable on the safe return of the vessel.

E Tony was going to come but cancelled when he realized the date would clash with his wife's birthday.

Answer [   ]

Question 23

John's 1990 salary was equal to three times his current salary. It was double what he earned in 1993. Which piece of information do you require in order to establish the percentage decrease he has had to endure since 1990?

A Inflation over the period totalled 13 per cent.

B John paid £5,250 tax in 1990.

C The difference between John's salary in 1990 and 1993 totalled £7,000.

D The rate of tax in 1990 was 25 per cent.

E John's total current salary is only £1,750 greater than his 1990 tax bill.

Answer _____

Question 24

Peter lives on a small island a short distance from the mainland. His journey to work involves a boat trip and a train journey. Which two pieces of information do you require in order to establish the distance between Peter's house and the railway station?

A The channel between the island and the mainland is 300 yards across.

B It is exactly 100 metres from Peter's house to the pub.

C The railway station is on the shore and Peter can see it from his front garden.

D The locations of the house, pub and railway station form an equilateral triangle.

E The only other building on Peter's island is a pub.

Answer _____

Question 25

Donna, Lucy and Chris between them own 80 marbles. Which two pieces of information allow you to establish how many of the marbles are Chris's?

A Chris and Lucy have the same number.

B Donna owns twice as many as Lucy.

C Lucy used to have 25 until she gave some to her brother.

D Fred, Lucy's brother, has three fewer than twice as many as Donna.

Answer _____

Question 26

A piece of gold weighing 38 grams is not pure but mixed with base metals. Which three pieces of information do you need to establish the current market value of gold?

A   Eighty per cent of the weight is due to the base metal.

B   The base metal is copper.

C   To convert from grams to ounces, multiply by 0.03527.

D   The volume of the piece is 3 cubic centimetres.

E   Gold is worth £200 an ounce.

Answer

Question 27

Steven, Kathy and Gino are all to drive from their home to Springville for an evening out. Gino in his GTI drives at 100 mph, Kathy in her 2CV more sensibly averages 35 mph, while Steven never exceeds the speed limit of 60 mph. Which item of information do you require to establish the distance between their home town and Springville?

A   Gino arrived in Springville 5 minutes before Steven and 10 minutes before Kathy.

B   Despite all the stops at traffic lights, Kathy completed the journey in 35 minutes.

C   Gino was booked for speeding.

D   Steven completed the journey in 30 minutes.

Answer

Question 28

The town hall can accommodate 40 rows of seats with between 25 and 37 seats per row. Which three items of information do you require to establish the percentage of the town's population that can be seated in the town hall when full?

A   20 rows can hold over 28 seats.

B   The 1991 Census recorded the town as having a population of 22,350.

C   The front 30 rows hold a total of 780 seats (an average of 26 per row).

D   Since the closure of the shoe factory and the loss of 1,800 jobs, people have moved away, leaving the population now 7% below the census total.

E   In 1991, 18 per cent of the population were under five years of age.

F   The overall average number of seats per row is 28.

Answer [   ]

Question 29

Ford sells its basic 'Model T' at $4,250, or with extras for $5,050. Which item of information do you require to establish the most profitable option?

A   The price difference between options totals £800.

B   Ford aims at achieving a profit margin of 3 per cent.

C   The current basic model comes as standard with items sold as extras 18 months ago.

D   The basic model achieves the 3 per cent profit margin.

E   Competition with Japanese car manufacturers means that Ford has to supply the extras to customers at cost price.

Answer [   ]

Question 30

In her will, Claire's instructions state that all her possessions are to be sold and the cash shared out as follows: her second child is to receive £1,000 more than her third child, while her first-born is to get three times as much as her second. Which three items of information are required to establish how much Martin is to receive?

A   Sue received £3,500.

B   Claire had four children.

C   Martin is 18 months older than Sue and one year younger than Peter.

D   Ken, Claire's youngest, was born two years after Sue.

E   The children mentioned in the will are called Sue, Peter and Martin.

F   Tragically, Claire outlived one of her children.

Answer [   ]

End of test

Numerical test 4: Practice intermediate-level data interpretation test

This type of question provides numerical data with between two and four questions relating to it which you must answer. It may pay to look at the suggested answers prior to attempting lengthy calculations as it is sometimes possible to rule some of them out and to estimate the correct answer by rounding up sums to more convenient figures. If you do not have sufficient time to finish, try an educated guess. Each suggested answer is given a number. To record your answer you simply mark the answer in the answer box.

This test comprises 25 questions and you are allowed 25 minutes to complete it.

The table below indicates the total number of young people and what they did after leaving school in the rural districts of an English county between the years 1988 and 1991.

Year	1988	1989	1990	1991
No of school leavers	3,000	2,196	2,400	1,652
Returned to education	450	769	480	798
Entered employment	300	285	240	189
Entered training	600	483	480	266
Became unemployed	750	373	480	147
Left district	150	66	120	189
Unknown	750	220	600	63

1   Between the years 1988 and 1990, which after-school activity saw the greatest percentage increase?

   1) returned to education   2) entered training

   3) became unemployed   4) left the district

   Answer [   ]

2   How many activities were selected by the same percentage of young people in 1988 and 1990?

   1) two categories   2) four categories

   3) five categories   4) three categories

   Answer [   ]

3   How many times more popular was returning to education compared with entering training in 1991?

   1) five times   2) six times   3) four times   4) three times

   Answer [   ]

4   Over the four-year period, what was the average number of annual school leavers?

   1) 2,309   2) 3,216   3) 2,312   4) 2,038

   Answer [   ]

The table below illustrates the population structures of countries. The data relate to January 1990.

Country	Total population (millions)	Live births per 1,000	Deaths per 1,000
Country A	56.4	13.2	11.9
Country B	53.6	12.9	12.3
Country C	70.3	11.7	11.6
Country D	12.7	9.9	10.1
Country E	18.2	10.8	11.2

5   Which country is experiencing the fastest rate of growth in population?

1) A   2) B   3) C   4) E

Answer

6   Which country's population is over four times smaller than country B's?

1) A   2) B   3) C   4) D

Answer

7   Which country experienced just over 125,000 births?

1) B   2) C   3) D   4) E

Answer

8   Which two countries experienced a mean rate of death per thousand of 11.55?

1) A and B   2) A and E   3) A and C   4) D and E

Answer

The table below shows the monthly average rainfall, hours of sunshine and wind speed for a European country. Consult it to answer the questions below.

	Rainfall (mm)	Sunshine (hours)	Wind speed (knots)
January	91	54	21
February	108	80	17
March	155	140	15
April	160	153	13
May	121	165	12
June	97	228	9
July	88	218	10
August	80	200	11
September	113	193	12
October	102	120	15
November	114	90	16
December	103	64	18

(9)   What is the mean wind speed for the months of January, February and March?

1) 18.11   2) 16.66   3) 17.66   4) 15.33

Answer _____

10   Which three consecutive months have a total of 403 hours of sunshine?

1) May, June, July   2) October, November, December

3) March, April, May   4) September, October, November

Answer _____

11   Identify the percentage that expresses the increase in sunshine between the months of February and March.

1) 75%   2) 8%   3) 16%   4) 50%

Answer _____

12   What is the ratio between the rainfall during the wettest and driest months?

1) 2:1   2) 1:2   3) 1:3   4) 3:1

Answer

The table below shows population, infant mortality, birth rate and agricultural area per person for five countries.

Country	Population (millions)	Infant mortality per 1,000 births	Total number of births per 1,000	Agricultural area per person (acres)
1980				
A	10	45	12	0.25
B	6	82	24	0.125
C	50	11	9	0.1
D	3	30	16	1.3
E	21	60	19	0.9
1990				
A	12	33	11	–
B	6.5	68	24	–
C	49	7	9	–
D	3.1	26	18	–
E	23	45	21	–

Key: – = Information not available

13   Which country experienced the highest rate of infant mortality in 1990?

1) E   2) A   3) B   4) C

Answer

14   Which countries have experienced an increase of two births per 1,000 over the decade?

1) E and D   2) A and C   3) B and C   4) D and A

Answer

15 What is the percentage increase in population experienced by country E over the decade illustrated?

1) 10.5%   2) 8.5%   3) 9.0%   4) 9.5%

Answer

16 If in country A the same amount of agricultural land is in use in 1990 as was the case in 1980, to what does the agricultural area per person decrease in 1990 (suggested answers are rounded down to two decimal places)?

1) 0.20   2) 0.15   3) 0.30   4) none of these

Answer

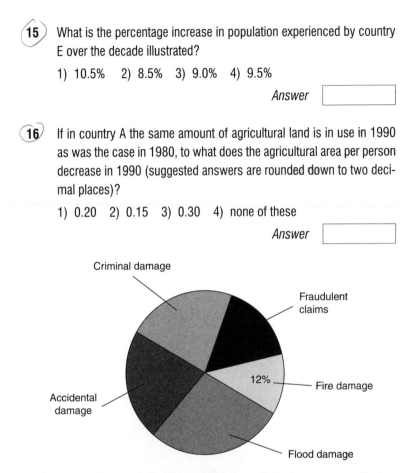

FIGURE 6   Nature of all claims against the unlucky insurance syndicate

17 If all flood, accidental and criminal damage related claims totalled 72%, how many fraudulent claims would you expect among a total of 2,500 claims in all?

1) 200   2) 300   3) 400   4) 500

Answer

18 Express the frequency of claims from fire damage against all genuine claims as a ratio in its simplest form (take genuine claims = all claims − fraudulent claims).

1) 4:20   2) 25:3   3) 3:25   4) cannot tell

Answer

19   If the fire damage claims totalled $420,000 and the number of all claims was 7,000, what would be the average value of the fire damage claims?

1) 500

2) 700

3) 900

4) 1,100

Answer [   ]

20   What would be the angle of the criminal damage segment of the pie if it represented 20% of all claims?

1) 66 degrees

2) 68 degrees

3) 70 degrees

4) 72 degrees

Answer [   ]

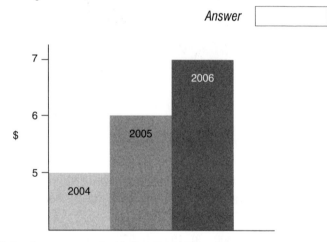

FIGURE 7   Average wage in the Free Trade Economic Zone

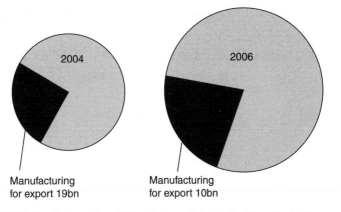

Manufacturing
for export 19bn

Manufacturing
for export 10bn

FIGURE 8 Dollar value (billions) by activity in the Free Trade Economic Zone

21 How would the $ axis on the graph usually be labelled?

1) x   2) y   3) –x   4) –y

Answer

22 For every cent increase in the average wage, what has been the gain/ loss in the value of trade in manufacturing for export (take 1 bn = 1,000 million, and $1 = 100 cents)?

1) gain of 4.5 million   2) loss of 450 million

3) loss of 45 million   4) gain of 90 million

Answer

23 The average wage in fair trade in 2004 was:

1) $5 hourly   2) $5 daily   3) $5 weekly   4) cannot tell

Answer

24 In 2004 what was the total value of trade in the economic zone if manufacturing for export contributed 5% of that total?

1) 19   2) 92   3) 190   4) 380

Answer

25   If the total value of trade was 150 bn in 2006, calculate the angle of the manufacturing for export segment of the pie chart:

1) 22 degrees   2) 23 degrees   3) 24 degrees   4) cannot tell

Answer [   ]

End of test

Numerical test 5: Advanced data interpretation practice test

I [a graduate candidate] recently sat an advanced 'professional level' numerical test. The questions required candidates to extract data from multiple data sets (eg bar charts, pie charts, profit and loss account) and then to work through up to four calculations to reach the answer, combining relevant data from the respective data sets. Some of the questions tested understanding of data sufficiency – allowing you to answer 'true', 'false' or 'cannot say'.

This test comprises 23 questions that require a medium to high command of the numerical competencies examined in graduate psychometric tests. You are only allowed 23 minutes in which to attempt these questions (that is obviously 1 minute a question). Some of the questions will take longer than 1 minute to complete, so you should aim to answer the easier questions in less than 1 minute in order to spend more time on the more demanding questions. As with a real graduate test of numerical skills, few candidates will succeed in answering all the questions in the time allowed.

There are two styles of question.

Style 1

You are presented with data in the form of a table, graph or chart and must use the information to select one of the suggested answers to the series of questions that follow.

Style 2

You are given a passage to read, followed by a series of questions that comprise a statement relating to the passage. It is your task to say whether the statement is true or false or whether it is not possible to say whether the statement is true or false. You should base your decision only on the information or opinions given in the passage.

You should judge the statement to be true only if, for example, it can be calculated from the information given in the passage, it follows logically from the passage, it is a rewording of something contained in the passage or it is a valid summary of the passage or a part of it.

You should judge the statement to be false if, for example, it can be calculated from information given in the passage that it is wrong, if it cannot follow logically from the passage or if it contradicts something contained in the passage.

If you require more information than is contained in the passage before you can perform a calculation to test the statement or before you can tell whether the statement is true or false, then you should record your answer as 'cannot tell'.

You should work quickly and not spend too long on any one question. Work without interruption.

Do not use a calculator.

The table below shows the average propensity to save for three countries.

Country	Month	Savings ($)/asp	Income ($)
1	Jan	8	400
	Feb	120	600
	Mar	35	700
2	Jan	50	1,200
	Feb	45	900
	Mar	50	800
3	Jan	0.05 (asp)	1,100
	Feb	0.02 (asp)	7,700
	Mar	0.03 (asp)	6,600

1 What is the average propensity to save (aps) in the month of January for country 1 (savings/income = aps)?

50   0.02   25   0.2   5

Answer [   ]

2 Calculate the aps for the three-month period for country 2.

0.02   0.03   0.04   0.05

Answer [   ]

3 By how much would savings increase in the month of January in country 3 if incomes were to increase by $400 and the aps were to remain the same?

$100 $75 $55 $20 $5.5

Answer [   ]

4 Which country has the highest propensity to save in the month of March?

Country 1   Country 2   Country 3

Answer [   ]

Passage 1

Twenty-four billion pounds is invested in Premium Bonds and in the past 10 years the number of bonds in the draw has multiplied by seven. The chances of winning have recently changed from 27,500 to 1 to 24,000 to 1. Record sales have meant that a new machine to select winning numbers randomly was required. The predecessor took 50 minutes to complete the draw, while the new machine can complete the task in half that time. Each month there are 1 million winners.

5 The new machine identifies 40,000 winners a minute.

   True   False   Cannot tell

                            Answer [   ]

6 Ten years ago there was £4 billion invested in Premium Bonds.

   True   False   Cannot tell

                            Answer [   ]

7 Twenty-four billion pounds means twenty-four thousand million.

   True   False   Cannot tell

                            Answer [   ]

The table below shows extracts from the six-monthly cash-flow forecast for small company 'doing much better'.

	Jan	Feb	Mar	Apr	May	Jun	Total
Income $000							
Opening balance	(20)	(15.7)	(10.2)	(5.6)	(3.1)	0.6	
Sales receipts	17	19	22	14	16	17	105
Cash available	(3)	3.3	11.8	8.4	12.9	17.6	
Expenditure $000							
Net wages	3.0	3.0	3.0	3.0	3.0	3.0	18.0
NI/pensions			2.7			2.7	5.4
Direct costs	6.8	7.6	8.8	5.6	6.4	6.8	42.0

	Jan	Feb	Mar	Apr	May	Jun	Total
Marketing/sales/ telephone/computer	0.7	0.7	0.7	0.7	0.7	0.7	4.2
Transport/travel	0.4	0.4	0.4	0.4	0.4	0.4	2.4
Rent/business rates	1.2	1.2	1.2	1.2	1.2	1.2	7.2
Professional fees	0.6	0.6	0.6	0.6	0.6	0.6	3.6
Total expenditure	12.7	13.5	17.4	12.3	12.3	15.4	83.6
Monthly + or (−)	4.3	5.5	4.6	3.7	3.7	1.6	

8 For how many months of the period covered by the cash flow is it forecast that the directors of 'doing much better' would need to arrange some kind of loan facility?

1   2   3   4   5   6

Answer [   ]

9 What percentage of the income from sales is expended on direct costs?

25%   30%   35%   40%   45%

Answer [   ]

10 Express total expenditure on net wages and direct cost as a ratio in its lowest form.

7:3   4:6   6:4   3:7   3:7

Answer [   ]

11 Were the cash flow to be extended to include the month of July, what would be the opening balance for that month?

$1,600   ($1,600) $2,200   ($2,200) $1,000

Answer [   ]

12   If net wages were to increase to $8,000 during the months of April, May and June, by how much would you expect expenditure on NI/pensions to increase in June?

$7,200 $6,300 $5,400 $4,500 $3,600

Answer   [   ]

Passage 2

The government wants 50 per cent of people aged 18–30 to go to university, and many of these new students are expected to study for shorter foundation degrees. These last for two years and combine study with hands-on experience while in paid relevant work. Already 20,000 people are taking foundation degrees, and half the courses available have over 50 students enrolled. Most foundation degrees are by distance learning and are part-time. While foundation degrees are not for the faint-hearted, they may appeal to many students who currently follow conventional university courses and who leave university with debts and then have to compete for a graduate-level job against foundation degree graduates with work-related experience.

13   The government wants half of all people aged 18–30 to study at university for a foundation degree.

True   False   Cannot tell

Answer   [   ]

14   Because foundation degrees are by distance learning and part-time, self-discipline and strong motivation are critical if the student is to succeed.

True   False   Cannot tell

Answer   [   ]

15   There are 200 foundation degree courses on which 50 or more students are enrolled.

True   False   Cannot tell

Answer   [   ]

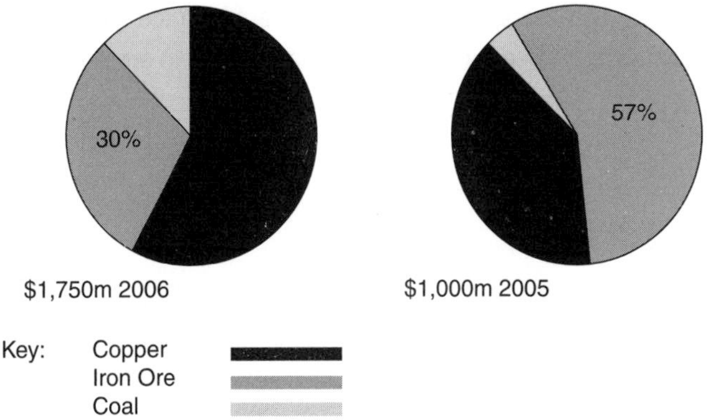

$1,750m 2006 $1,000m 2005

Key: Copper
        Iron Ore
        Coal

FIGURE 9   Analysis of contributions to gross profit by commodities

16   Over the two years, how much did coal contribute to gross profits?

$25m $40m $210m $250m $290m

Answer

17   If you take gross profit to equal revenue (from sales) minus cost of sales, then you can calculate the value of sales for 2005 from the given information.

True   False   Cannot tell

Answer

18   In real terms, how much more did iron ore contribute to the total gross profit in 2005 than in 2006?

$45m $46m $47m $48m $49m

Answer

19   In the context of the passage, gross profit means:

A   highest amount without accounting for costs, taxes or depreciation

B   figure remaining after all relevant deductions have been made

C   a percentage of revenue

D   total sales of the company for each year

E   none of these

Answer

20 For the two years, express in its simplest form the ratio between the contribution of coal and non-coal commodities to gross profit.

1:12   1:11   1:10   1:9   1:8

Answer

Passage 3

Head lice are parasitic insects that live on the hair close to the human scalp and feed on blood. At any one time it is estimated that one in four children aged between 4 and 11 are suffering an infection. A louse lives for about 300 days and a female will lay over 2,000 eggs. Girls and boys are infected at a ratio of three to one. Lice cannot fly or jump. Girls are more prone to infection because their play tends to involve prolonged contact between heads. Children in urban schools are more likely to be infected, but the reason for this is unknown.

21 Examine an eight-year-old child's head in an urban school and there is a one in four chance of finding head lice.

True   False   Cannot tell

Answer

22 You would expect the ratio of infection for girls and boys to be the same in an urban and a rural school.

True   False   Cannot tell

Answer

23 It can be inferred from the passage that infections occur when lice crawl from one head to another.

True   False   Cannot tell

Answer

End of test

Comment on your score in Test 5

A score of 15 or more

If you are applying for a graduate position at one of the top banks or consultancies, then this is the only score that you can be content with. From my experience, a score over 15 should see you through to the next stage in the recruitment process, but this will vary from campaign to campaign and, like most things, is not a certainty.

A score between 10 and 14

This is a very wide category of score and will include the near-miss candidate as well as someone who did only moderately well. So, decide where you believe you are on this scale and set about a systematic programme of practice in order to improve your score.

How you interpret your score will of course depend on what you are applying for, and if you are seeking a non-financial position then it is possible that this score band will be sufficient to see you through. If you are applying for a financial position, then get down to some more practice under realistic test conditions. I have suggested suitable sources of such practice material at other points in the book.

A score below 10

You run the real risk of being judged a great candidate except for the maths! Employers are increasingly looking for all-round candidates, and this includes a reasonable numerical competency. Reflect on the reason for your score. Did you spend too long on questions and so run out of time before you could attempt sufficient questions? Do you need to improve your accuracy when working quickly under the pressure of an exam? Once you have settled on the cause, then either set about a programme of revision to master the key operations and/or practise more under realistic practice conditions. Above all else, do not give up. Keep working at it and you will witness a marked improvement in your performance in numerical tests.

CHAPTER 4

English usage, reading comprehension and critical reasoning

These tests are my worst nightmare. I have a 2:1 degree and work experience but I feel freaked out by them.

(A graduate candidate)

I do really well in numerical tests but little better than the norm in verbal tests. Most companies are looking for candidates to achieve good scores in both and don't compensate a good score in one for a bad score in the other.

(Another graduate candidate)

If you concur with either of these sentiments, then rest assured that practice will help you to cope with nerves and will lead to a better score in these very common tests of ability.

I don't mean to overdo this point, as the real tests you face will have been designed and gone over very carefully, but the first thing to realize about verbal tests is that they lack the certainty of a numerical test. Language is more flexible and relative. In a maths test there is definitely a right answer and the rest are wrong, whereas in every verbal test there will be some candidate or another who feels that they have chosen an answer that is more correct than the one the test author suggests. You just have to accept that there is less certainty in verbal tests. When a test author is designing a high-level verbal test, he or she has to draw very fine distinctions between the suggested answers, much finer distinctions than we drawn in normal English usage. In some cases these distinctions can become so fine that they seem arbitrary, and to some extent they are; after all, it is not how we use language in the real world. They are obviously not this subjective, but think of them as a bit like a creative writing competition. In verbal tests, like a creative writing test, you sometimes have to learn to answer the questions according to the judge's view of what is right – and remember that the judge's decision is final!

A common error in the reading comprehension and critical reasoning tests is to err too much towards the 'cannot tell' suggested answer. In these tests you are typically given a passage and a series of questions or statements to which you must answer 'true', 'false' or 'cannot tell'. It is normal for the test instructions to advise you not to bring your own opinions or views to the exercise and to rely instead on the information contained in the passage. This simply means avoid relying on your own specialist knowledge or opinions to decide on the answer. What it does not mean is that you should be like some Cartesian and start to question everything. You need to arrive at a sensible balance and not apply too strict or too inflexible a test of proof.

It is important that you learn to pick up clues from the wording of the question or statement. If, for example, the question refers to 'a valid inference' or 'a premise', or asks 'is it necessarily the case…?', then by all means put on your logician's hat and apply strict criteria as to what can be deduced. However, if the question asks, for example, 'is it reasonable…?', 'on the balance of probability', 'might the author…?', then adjust your criterion accordingly and be prepared to apply a less strict test.

Practice will make a big difference to your approach to and performance in verbal tests. Set aside the necessary time, get hold of sufficient practice questions and allow yourself to become familiar with the typical demands placed on you in these common tests.

If English is not your first language

You are going to find some parts of every verbal test (in English) a greater challenge than a native speaker, so you need to adjust your programme of revision accordingly.

It is likely that the types of tests you will find most difficult are the reading comprehension and critical reading type questions. You might actually find yourself at an advantage in tests of English usage. This is because many native speakers of English have forgotten or never formally learned the rules of English grammar, while you will have.

To meet the challenge at an early stage, spend time reading quality newspapers and journals – if possible, daily. Doing so will help build your vocabulary and improve your proficiency at assimilating the meanings of the complex sentences and sentence structures that occur in the passages in these tests. Look up unfamiliar words. Practise writing 70-word reviews of articles found in these publications.

If you suffer from a disability

If your ability to undertake any psychometric test could be adversely affected by a disability, then speak to the employer to which you are applying straight away and seek their advice on how your requirements can best be accommodated. Provide full details of your condition and be clear on the special arrangements you require. You may be allowed extra time or a test reader or someone to record your answers. Braille or large-text versions of the test may be made available.

It is reasonable to expect your requirements to be given proper consideration and, wherever possible, accommodated. Evidence of your condition may be required. Be sure to raise your needs at an early stage in order that the organizers have time to accommodate them and so that you have sufficient time to obtain any formal proof of your condition that they may require.

In your search for work you are bound to come across SHL, a leading publisher of graduate tests including verbal ability tests. SHL's graduate products include:

- ability screening online;
- Fastrack;
- MGIB (Management and Graduate Item Bank).

SHL has an extensive client list, and giants like L'Oréal, Colgate-Palmolive, Ford, Sony, Philips, KraftFoods, Ericsson, Vodafone and many others use its psychometric products.

English usage

To write or speak English, or for that matter any natural language, involves rules of usage called grammar. To speak or write correctly you do not need to recite these rules. Grammar classes at school can be distant, possibly a bad memory, and the content of these lessons long forgotten. To speak or write correctly all that is required is that you apply the rules correctly – that you implicitly follow the rules.

In the context of psychometric tests, however, the correct application of the rules is insufficient. To do well in these tests you have to know the rules as well as follow them. For most candidates this means a certain amount of revision. It is well worth the effort. The candidate who knows the rules will be far more confident, will better realize what is behind the examiners' questions and will recognize the significance of the possibly subtle differences in the suggested questions.

What follows is a statement of the rules of English relevant to psychometric tests. The practice questions and tests that follow the glossary allow you to put the rules into practice.

At the intermediate level you will find more practice at this sort of question in the following Kogan Page testing titles:

Verbal Reasoning Tests, Workbook
Ultimate Psychometric Tests, 2nd edition
How to Pass Advanced Verbal Reasoning Tests, 2nd edition

Glossary

Adjective

An adjective adds detail to a noun or pronoun. To say, for example, that 'the record was scratched' is to add the adjective 'scratched' to the noun 'record'.

Adjectives can also limit or define. For this reason it is proper to think of them as modifiers. For example, if we say that 'Few people enjoy the game', the adjective 'few' limits rather than describes the noun 'people'.

Adverb

An adverb modifies a verb. It can detail, limit or define. If we say, for example, 'The yacht was sinking fast', the adverb 'fast' adds detail to the verb 'sinking'. 'Not' and 'very' are adverbs. An adverb can also add detail to an adjective ('very few') or another adverb ('very fast').

Note that adjectives and adverbs can be either phrases or words. In the statement 'The people opposite me enjoyed the game', the phrase 'opposite me' limits the noun 'people', so is an adjective.

Apposition

An appositional word or phrase is a noun or pronoun placed next to another noun or pronoun. It has the same meaning, but its function is to rename or identify the subject. For example, if I were to say 'The child, Junior, drank all the milk', I would be introducing a one-word apposition: 'Junior'. An example of an appositional phrase is 'a one-year-old' in the statement 'The child, a one-year-old, drank all the milk'.

Article

Articles modify nouns. They are either indefinite or definite. 'A' and 'an' are indefinite articles because they modify a singular noun that is general. The article 'the' is particular, so is used to modify a particular noun.

Clause

A clause is a group of words within a sentence which contains a subject and a verb. If you were to say, for example, 'They bought the camera in order to photograph the baby' you have two clauses: first clause, 'They bought the camera' (subject 'camera', verb 'bought'); second clause, 'in order to photograph the baby' (subject 'baby', verb 'photograph').

There are two types of clause:

Main clause

A main clause expresses a complete thought and makes sense on its own. The example 'They bought the camera' is a main clause.

Subordinate clause

A subordinate clause on its own does not make sense or express a complete thought. 'In order to photograph the baby' is an example of a subordinate clause.

Complement

The basic parts of a sentence are a subject, a verb and a complement. The complement follows the subject and verb to complete the meaning. It can be any word or phrase. For example:

> 'Scott went on holiday' (The complement is the noun 'holiday', 'Scott' the subject and 'went' the verb.)
>
> 'Describe the taste to me.' (The complement is the pronoun 'me', 'taste' the subject, and 'describe' the verb.)

Conjunction

A conjunction is a word that joins words, phrases or clauses. A conjunction can either treat clauses equally or make one more important. A coordinating conjunction connects without making either part more important, and usually involves a comma being placed before the conjunction. Examples are 'or', 'for', 'but' and 'nor'. A subordinating conjunction makes the clause it begins less important. Examples are 'as', 'because', 'when' and 'which'.

Direct object

A direct object is a complement to which the verb in a sentence is directed. It is either a noun or a pronoun, phrase or clause. In the examples provided in the entry for 'Complement', the words 'holiday' and 'me' are both direct objects of the verbs 'went' and 'describe' respectively.

Gerund

A gerund is used as a noun but is formed from a verb (so it is a verbal; see below). It ends in '-ing' and often begins a phrase. For example:

> 'Playing all day was exhausting.' (The gerund is 'playing', formed from the verb 'to play' but used in this context as a noun.)
>
> 'Smoking causes cancer.'
>
> 'She loves cycling in the open countryside.' (In this instance, the gerund is not at the beginning of the sentence.)

Indirect object

A sentence that contains an indirect object must also contain a direct object because the former indicates to whom or what the action of the verb is directed. Like a direct object, an indirect object is a complement. For example, take the sentence 'Thomas wanted the videos for his students'. In this case the subject is 'Thomas', the verb 'wanted', the direct object 'the videos' and the indirect object 'his students'.

Infinitive

An infinitive consists of the word 'to' followed by a verb used as either a noun, an adjective or an adverb. For example:

'To smile is bliss' (the verb 'to smile' is here used as a noun).

'If only you were to smile' (the verb 'to smile' is here being used as an adverb).

Watch out for split infinitives. A split infinitive has an adverb placed between the 'to' and the verb. A famous example is 'to boldly go'. To avoid splitting the infinitive the phrase should read 'to go boldly'.

Modifier

A modifier adds information and may take the form of a word, a phrase or a clause. Adjectives, adverbs and articles are examples of modifiers.

Misplaced modifier

A modifier is misplaced if, in a sentence, it modifies the wrong word; if it seems to describe a thing or person other than the thing or person it should describe. To correct the situation, you simply move the modifier. For example: 'The reporter went to the press briefing to hear about the escaped lion with a tape recorder.' This should have read: 'The reporter with a tape recorder went to the press briefing to hear about the escaped lion.'

Dangling modifier

A modifier is said to dangle if it cannot be attached to the subject of the main clause, so unless the sentence is changed it has nothing to modify. For example:

> 'Before writing a press release, the reader should be considered.' The phrase 'Before writing a press release' is a dangling modifier because it does not have a subject to modify. To correct the situation the sentence would have to be changed so that it read, for example, 'Before writing a press release, the writer should consider the reader.'

Noun

A noun is a word, a clause or a phrase that identifies a person, a place, an idea or a thing. There are five types of noun:

Proper noun

A proper noun names a particular person, place or thing. Examples of proper nouns are 'Tony', 'Frances' and 'Taj Mahal'. Note that proper nouns always begin with a capital letter.

Common noun

A common noun identifies a general thing, a place or a kind of person, for example 'house', 'village green' or 'traffic warden'.

Collective noun

Collective nouns are singular but they identify groups of individuals, for example 'audience', 'class' and 'crowd'.

Concrete noun

Concrete nouns identify inanimate objects such as 'mineral', 'metal', 'paper' and 'feather'. Common nouns can also be concrete nouns; for example, chair and table are both common and concrete nouns.

Abstract noun

Abstract nouns identify qualities and ideals such as 'truth', 'justice' and 'intelligence'.

Participle

A participle is formed from a verb that is used like an adjective. A present participle ends in '-ing', while a past participle usually ends in '-ed', '-en' or '-t'. An example of a present participle is 'barking' in the sentence: 'The barking dog kept John awake.' An example of a past participle is 'celebrated' in the sentence: 'The celebrated climber gave a speech.'

Watch out for dangling participial phrases. A participial phrase begins with a participle. It is dangling if there is no noun or pronoun to which it adds detail. For example, the following statement contains a dangling participial phrase:

'Having finished the crossword, the dog went out into the garden.'

The participial phrase 'Having finished the crossword' is dangling because there is no sensible noun or pronoun to which it relates. To make the statement sensible, you would need to provide a noun or pronoun. For example:

'Having finished the crossword, Thomas went out into the garden with the dog.'

Parts of speech

There are eight basic types of word: nouns, pronouns, verbs, adjectives, adverbs, prepositions, conjunctions and interjectives.

Pronoun

A pronoun can be used in place of a noun. For example:

'The water was warm, and it remained so all day.'

The pronoun 'it' has been used in this sentence in place of the noun 'water'.

When replacing nouns with pronouns you must take care that you do not introduce ambiguity. For example: 'The water remained warm all day and it was the warmest I can remember'. In this instance it is unclear whether it is the water or the day that was the warmest in memory. When there is a risk of ambiguity, the noun should be repeated. For example, in the above case the ambiguity is removed if we write: 'The water remained warm all day, the warmest day I can remember'.

There are a great many types of pronoun and they are classified by function. The list here is not exhaustive:

Demonstrative pronouns:	this, that, these, those
Interrogative pronouns:	which, who, whom, what, whose
Personal pronouns:	I, he, you, she, us, them
Possessive pronouns:	my, mine, your, its, his, her, our, their
Indefinite pronouns:	all, both, few, many, some

Sentence

A sentence must have a subject and a verb and express a complete thought. For example, the statement 'Opera began' has a subject ('Opera') and a verb ('began') but does not express a complete thought, so is not a sentence. The situation is easily corrected if we write, 'The opera began', as this does express a complete thought and so is a sentence.

'They cried' is an example of a sentence that comprises no more than a subject and a verb yet still expresses a complete thought.

Sentences are classified according to what they express or by their structure. In the context of psychometric tests, their classification according to structure is more relevant.

Sentences can be classified under four types of structure, as follows.

Simple sentences

A simple sentence comprises one main clause only, so remember that a main clause can be a sentence. Examples are usually short, for instance 'She hates grammar'; but they need not be, as the following example illustrates:

'The assistant editor made over 20 suggested alterations in the first few pages of text.'

Compound sentences

A compound sentence has two or more main clauses. For example:

First main clause:	'Come and see our range of mountain bikes
Connective:	and
Second main clause:	we will be pleased to demonstrate any model.'

Complex sentences

A complex sentence comprises one main clause and one or more subordinate clauses. For example:

Subordinate clause:	'After having a bath
Main clause:	Thomas felt a lot better.'

Compound complex sentences

Compound complex sentences comprise two or more main clauses and one or more subordinate clauses. For example:

First main clause:	'Thomas so enjoyed the opera
First subordinate clause:	which he had heard was good
Second main clause:	that he vowed to go each week,
Second subordinate clause:	assuming he could obtain tickets.'

In English usage tests, look out for two or more sentences that are joined by a comma or have no punctuation separating them. For example: 'The sun shone, they were very happy.' This kind of error is often examined and can be corrected with a full stop, a semicolon or the use of the conjunction 'and' in place of the comma.

Another commonly tested error involves a phrase or subordinate clause being presented as a sentence.

Subject

A subject is the word or words being talked about in the sentence. A subject is often a noun but can be a pronoun, a verbal noun (but not a participle), a phrase or clause. A subject has one or more verbs that tell what the subject is doing. The subject is underlined in the following sentences:

Oystercatchers are black and white wading birds.' (subject as a noun)

'After showering, she went to work.' (subject as a pronoun)

'Rain making is impossible.' (subject as a gerund phrase)

'What is happening is quite the most extraordinary thing imaginable.' (subject as a subordinate clause)

Tense

Tense shows the moment to which a verb refers. A simple tense can show the past, present or future, for example 'he swam', 'he swims', 'he will swim'. What are called perfect tenses can be further subdivided (notice that all three contain past participles):

Present perfect tense

The present perfect shows that an action that began in the past is continuing or has been completed in the present, for example 'Birthdays are always celebrated.'

Past perfect tense

The past perfect (or pluperfect) tense shows that an action was completed before a past point in time, for example 'Gino had finished his birthday celebration by midnight.'

Future perfect tense

The future perfect tense shows that a future action will be completed after another future action, for example 'By the time this book is published, my first child will have been born.' In a verbal usage exam, always check that the tenses of a sentence are not mixed up. In particular, ensure that the verb in the subordinate clause has the same tense as the verb in the main clause.

Verb

A verb tells what someone, or something, is or does, its state or condition. There are two types of action verb, transitive and intransitive.

In 'She <u>publishes</u> books', 'publishes' is transitive because it is followed by a direct object. In 'The river <u>winds</u> through the hills', 'winds' is intransitive as it is not followed by a direct object. There are also linking verbs, for example 'The sea <u>looks</u> green' and 'she <u>is</u> accomplished' – these tell us what someone or something is.

Questions in selection tests are sometimes on the characteristics of verbs, in particular the number, person and tense of verbs.

Number
A verb must agree with the number of its subject. If the subject is plural, so is the verb. 'Mother and baby does well' is incorrect because the subject is plural while the verb is singular.

Person
A verb can be in the first, second or third person (singular or plural) and serves to establish whether or not the subject is speaking, being addressed or being spoken about. The same verb form often applies to different persons or numbers:

'We <u>won</u> the race.' (plural first person)
'You <u>won</u> the race.' (singular or plural second person)
'They <u>won</u> the race.' (plural third person)

Tense
Tense shows whether or not the verb refers to the past, present or future. The verb of any subordinate clause must agree with the tense of the main clause. For example, the sentence 'After he read the paper, Jon asks anyone else if they would like to read it', is incorrect because the verb in the main clause is in the present tense while the verb in the subordinate clause is in the past tense.

Verbal
A verbal is derived from a verb but is not used as such. Verbals are, instead, used as either nouns, adjectives or infinitives. See *Gerund*, *Participle* and *Infinitive* for examples.

Now practise these rules by attempting the following questions.

One hundred and thirty-five practice questions

CUT-E

The test publisher cut-e assesses over 2 million people per year in over 70 countries and 20 languages. Its online tests and questionnaires are used by, for example, IKEA, Nestlé, Vodafone and Siemens. The company offers the usual numerical, verbal logical and spatial reasoning sub-tests and an English language proficiency test which examines fluency and vocabulary.

Use the material in this chapter to prepare for cut-e's English language proficiency test and English usage tests like it.

Identify the correct sentences.

1 A There are redundancies when the managing director arrived.

B There will be redundancies after the managing director arrived.

C After the new managing director arrived, there were redundancies.

D After the new managing director arrived, there will be many redundancies.

E None of these.

Answer ☐

2 A As soon as the sales figures are available, the directors knew they had achieved their targets.

B As soon as the sales figures were available, the directors knew they had achieved their targets.

    C As soon as the sales figures are available, the directors knew they have achieved their targets.

    D None of these.   *Answer* [   ]

3 A Although the business plan looks promising, the bank manager suspected that the proposal is unlikely to succeed.

    B Although the business plan looks promising, the bank manager suspects the proposal was unlikely to succeed.

    C Although the business plan looked promising, the bank manager suspected that the proposal was unlikely to succeed.

    D None of these.   *Answer* [   ]

4 A If you were to contact the client you might find that they would buy.

    B If you are to contact the client you might find that they would buy.

    C If you were to contact the client you will find that they will buy.

    D None of these.   *Answer* [   ]

5 A While the photocopier is broken you will have to go across the road to the copy shop.

    B While the photocopier was broken you will have to go across the road to the copy shop.

    C When the photocopier is broken you went across the road to the copy shop.

    D None of these.   *Answer* [   ]

6 A My new colleague is the one who has the red car.

    B My new colleague was the one whom had the red car.

    C My new colleague will be the one who had the red car.

    D None of these.   *Answer* [   ]

7 A The family will be eating their meal in the restaurant.

B The family was eating its meal in the restaurant.

C The family were eating their meal in the restaurant.

D None of these.   *Answer* [   ]

8 A Neither you nor I is able to make sense of this.

B Neither you nor I are able to make sense of this.

C Neither you nor I will be able to make sense of this.

D None of these.   *Answer* [   ]

9 A Bill, as well as the rest of his colleagues, is going to the annual office dinner.

B Bill, as well as the rest of his colleagues, are going to the annual office dinner.

C Neither of these.   *Answer* [   ]

10 A You girls over there what do you think you are doing.

B You girl over there what do you think you are doing.

C Neither of these.   *Answer* [   ]

Identify any incorrect sentences. The error for which you are looking is a dangling participle phrase.

11 A Having read of the outbreak of unrest in Africa, Joe heard the next day that war had broke out.

B The Prime Minister decided to recall Parliament; he faced a sea of very grave faces when he rose to make his statement.

C Having read of the outbreak of unrest in Africa, the next day war broke out.

D None of these.   *Answer* [   ]

12 A Wishing the department to succeed, new staff were taken on.

   B It was clear that the Prime Minister had written off the by-election result; he intended to blame it on the recession.

   C Neither of these.   *Answer*

13 A After having finished the exam, the candidates felt a great sense of relief.

   B Feeling tired of the run, Hope decided to take a bath.

   C My mother accused me of being mad, talking to myself all the time.

   D None of these.   *Answer*

14 A The mosquitoes drove him mad, walking through the jungle.

   B When we got to the house, having walked for many hours, we simply fell into bed and slept.

   C Neither of these.   *Answer*

15 A Tests play an important role in the allocation of opportunities; their use, therefore, should be closely controlled.

   B Woken from sleep by the bright sunshine, Mary decided to get up straight away.

   C Beaten roundly in battle by the French army, the English decided to sue for peace.

   D None of these.   *Answer*

Split infinitives – identify the *incorrect* sentence.

16 A From the age of three it was clear that Alison was going to quickly go to the top of the class.

   B From the age of three it was clear that Alison was going to go quickly to the top of the class.

   C Neither of these.   *Answer*

17 A After going on her training course Susan was skilful in the way she managed to coordinate the concurrent sales and marketing conferences.

    B After going on her training course Susan was able to coordinate skilfully the concurrent sales and marketing conferences.

    C Neither of these.   *Answer*

18 A It was clear that to precipitately press ahead would have been a mistake.

    B It was clear that to press ahead precipitately would have been a mistake.

    C Neither of these.   *Answer*

19 A He wanted, at an accelerated pace, to move ahead, but his boss prevented him from doing so.

    B He wanted to move ahead at an accelerated pace, but his boss prevented him from doing so.

    C Neither of these.   *Answer*

20 A The sales team wished to really work hard in order to achieve its targets.

    B The sales team wished really to work hard in order to achieve its targets.

    C Neither of these.   *Answer*

21 A Hoping to make amends, therefore, the Prime Minister called a special meeting of her cabinet.

    B Hoping to, therefore, make amends the Prime Minister called a special meeting of his cabinet.

    C Neither of these.

                     Answer

The following sentences test your understanding of the use of *apostrophes*. Identify the *correct* sentences. Note that more than one sentence may be correct.

22 A It's a good thing you gave the baby lamb it's extra milk during the night.

    B It's a good thing you gave the baby lamb its extra milk during the night.

    C It is a good thing you gave the baby lamb its extra milk during the night.

    D None of these.   *Answer*

23 A Put the boys' shoes on otherwise their feet will get wet.

    B Put the boy's shoes on otherwise their feet will get wet.

    C Put the boys' shoes on otherwise his feet will get wet.

    D None of these.

                                Answer

24 A Miles's achievement at cricket will long be remembered at his old school.

    B Miles's achievements at cricket will long be remembered at his old school.

    C Mile's achievement at cricket will long be remembered at his old school.

    D None of these.   *Answer*

25 A The 1960s were a time when sexual liberation was first condoned.

    B The 1960's were a time when sexual liberation was first condoned.

    C The sixty's were a time when sexual liberation was condoned.

    D None of these.   *Answer*

26 A The forecast for todays weather predicts rain, but tomorrow it's going to be fine.

   B The forecast for today's weather predicts rain, but tomorrow its going to be fine.

   C The forecast for todays weather predicts rain, but tomorrow its going to be fine.

   D None of these.   *Answer* ☐

Some tests require you to decide between *parts of a sentence* and identify which is *correct*. With the following examples, your task is to identify which of the suggested parts complete the sentence correctly.

27 Central banks had to step in to prop up the European Exchange Rate Mechanism…

   A tomorrow if massive selling is not to threaten the French franc.

   B yesterday as massive selling threatened the French franc.

   C Neither of these.   *Answer* ☐

28 … cash offer under its recently announced enhanced dividend plan have come off best.

   A The shareholders who subscribed to the companys

   B The shareholder who subscribed for the company's

   C The shareholder who subscribed to the company's

   D None of these.   *Answer* ☐

29 Receivers were called in but they will attempt to keep the company trading…

   A it all depends on whether there are sufficient funds to pay salaries due on the last day of the month.

   B and decide whether the company has sufficient funds to pay the salaries due on the last day of the month.

   C if there are sufficient funds to pay this month's salaries.

   D None of these.   *Answer* ☐

30   … they were frequently amended to allow for individual projects to be approved.

A   Policy guidelines, agreed by the committee, however,

B   Policy guidelines were agreed by the committee,

C   Policy guidelines were agreed by the committee; however,

D   None of these.   *Answer*

31   … from the opposition when he called on them to change their minds and vote with the government.

A   He elicited a baying increase of support

B   He elated a tremendous increase in support

C   He elicited a baying crescendo of support

D   None of these.   *Answer*

Use of negatives

32   Only one of the following sentences is incorrect; which one is it?

A   'You don't want not to do that, do you?'

B   'I should not bother washing the car, dear,' said a wife to her husband, to which he replied, 'I can't not do it; it looks disgraceful.'

C   He was stopped by the beggar, but hadn't got any money.

D   You should not think there are no examples when killing could be warranted.

E   It's not impossible that we will be able to get away tonight before 7 o'clock.

                              Answer

Use of capitals

33 The capitalization of three of the following sentences is incorrect. Which sentences are they?

A person who comes from France will usually speak French.

B It was William Shakespeare who first coined the phrase 'all the world's a stage'.

C The Government buildings have all been renovated.

D After the management buy-out, Nicholas Smith took over as the new Managing Director.

E When asked which book he would take on his desert island, he said '*The Catcher in the Rye*'.

F Every morning we had to swear allegiance to the american flag.

G The Church situated on the corner is called The Church of St John.

H Sitting in the conference room was a group of managers, directors and other senior executives.

Answer [   ]

34 Which of the following include incomplete sentences or do not form complete sentences?

A He bought the Australian newspaper group. In order to complete his domination of the world's press.

B To err is human.

C 'Passing my driving test is my greatest achievement so far'. She said.

D The exhausted cyclist.

E She got tanned. And the sun shone at the weekend.

F Somewhere over the rainbow.

G Having worked, she now decided to retire.

Answer [   ]

Practice punctuation

35 Which of the following sentences is correctly punctuated?

    A For the sales conference, Alison had to check the seating, the lighting, the pen situation and the catering.

    B For the sales conference, Alison had to check the seating, the lighting, the pen situation, and the catering.

    C Neither sentence.   *Answer* [　　　　　]

36 A There were four boys chosen for the job; Toby, Scott, Miles and Mark.

    B There were four boys chosen for the job: Toby, Scott, Miles and Mark.

    C Neither sentence.   *Answer* [　　　　　]

37 A Although he could not be sure of his map reading, he decided to turn left at the next junction.

    B Although he could not be sure of his map reading he decided to turn left at the next junction.

    C Neither of these.

           Answer [　　　　　]

38 A Yes – he interjected, for he had to say exactly what he felt.

    B Yes; he interjected, for he had to say exactly what he felt.

    C Neither sentence.

           Answer [　　　　　]

39 A Max, Bill and Geoff were in the room. So which boy's hat is this?

    B Max, Bill and Geoff were in the room. So which boys' hat is this?

    C Neither sentence.   *Answer* [　　　　　]

40 A The M25 is to be made into a 16-lane highway, many local residents find this unacceptable.

B The M25 is to be made into a 16-lane highway; many local residents find this unacceptable.

C Neither sentence. *Answer* ☐

41 A He decided to become a full time student.

B He decided to become a full-time student.

C Neither sentence.

Answer ☐

42 A Would they need to ask the permission of the farmer to cross his land? it wasn't quite clear from the notice.

B Would they need to ask the permission of the farmer to cross his land; it wasn't clear from the notice.

C Neither sentence.

Answer ☐

43 A The MP, Crispin Biggs-Williams, was the first to declare his anti European intentions by waving his jacket – a brightly striped old Wellington blazer – and was first into the opposition lobby.

B The MP Crispin Biggs-Williams, was the first to declare his anti Europeans intentions by waving his jacket – a brightly striped old Wellington blazer – and was first into the opposition lobby.

C Neither sentence. *Answer* ☐

44 A 'I am enjoying this' – he said, dreamily.

B 'I'm enjoying this' – he said, dreamily.

C Neither sentence.

Answer ☐

Spelling

Underline the *correct* choice in the following sentences.

45 He was most complementary/complimentary about my new painting.

46 The effect/affect you had on the children was to excite them.

47 The tolling of the church bell, striking on the hour, every hour, was continuous/continual.

48 Before disciplinary action is taken, advise/advice should be offered to the member of staff.

49 By the time the starting pistol was fired, the runners were all ready/already for the race.

50 The birthday cake was divided among/between the many guests.

51 Children, put your toys back into/in to the toy-box.

52 You will find them either/(no word required) in the wardrobe, on the chair or in the chest of drawers.

53 After her engagement, she could not help but flout/flaunt her diamond ring at every opportunity.

54 For my holiday in Africa, I was reminded to take/bring my malaria tablets.

55 That case is quite different from/than the previous one we discussed.

56 Booking is not required for families with fewer/less than five members.

57 The pub is about half a mile farther/further down the road.

58 They will be delighted if Tony and I/me join them for lunch.

59 He had been lying/laying down for many hours before he was able to shake off his headache.

Word link

These questions comprise two lines of words, one above the other. On the top line are two words, while on the lower line there are six. Your task is to identify two words in the lower line, one in each half, which form an analogy when paired with the word in the upper line. You indicate your answer by underlining the two words on the lower line. Although an analogy is when the words are in some way similar, note that in some questions the connection between the words is that they are opposites.

Example questions

60 HOT   SPICY
        confront <u>sparse</u> attack   arrest <u>thin</u> ignore

The connection is that the words are synonyms.

61 FLAT   ROUGH
        <u>even</u> taxidermist hatchback   mouse house <u>rugged</u>

The connection in this case is that the words are opposites.

62 FAST   FEAST
        conversion rapid <u>diet</u>   <u>slow</u> gluttony waterfall

The connection is that the opposite of 'fast' is 'slow' and the opposite of 'feast' is 'diet', but note how the connections are made diagonally across the top and bottom line.

63 HORSE   CAR
        putter <u>rider</u> jump   pig <u>driver</u> cow

The connection in this example is that a horse has a rider and a car has a driver.

Practice questions

64 CRICKET
      golf locust vampire

BAT
grasshopper club grass

65 SAILOR
      hornpipe ship trumpet

SURGEON
xylophone hospital waltz

66 RUN
      sprint manage trot

CONTROL
walk regulate relax

67 HIGH
      intoxicate top above

LOW
buttock bottom beyond

68 CLOWN
      idiot king approximate

CIRCUS
roundabout palace pin

69 ASSEMBLE
      enjoy construct retreat

WITHDRAW
age retire superannuate

70 JUDGE
      date court horse

JOCKEY
bench club isotherm

71 CONCUR
      agree reject explain

ARGUE
propose dispute believe

72 KING
      kong emperor size

KINGDOM
empire penguin hall

73 RABBIT
      hearse horse hoarse

FUR
hair hare heir

74 YACHT
      care car dinghy

SAIL
truck petrol outboard

75 DAWN
      patrol stars light

SUNSET
moon boulevard dark

76 GOVERNMENT
      free anarchy conservative

CHAOS
liberal order command

77 SOCIALIST   ENVIRONMENTALIST
red blue black   yellow white green

78 CHINA   FRANCE
clay tea Asia   polish wine Europe

79 INEPT   PERFECT
complete apt competent   whole exodus defective

80 DRAWS   ASSESSES
sketches sledge attractions   praises amalgamate appraises

81 NORTH   SOUTH
Wales Scotland west   Sussex Kent east

82 CONGESTION   INFERENCE
blockage superior infection   guess inferior conclusion

83 DYE   TAN
cloth funeral shoe   coffin leather brown

84 METAL   COIN
wood paper percussion   brass note news

85 SEASONABLE   RESPECTABLE
untimely decreasing winter   upright pepper disgraceful

86 CENTIMETRE   INCH
metre meter meat   foot claw gas

87 WEAK   GREEN
month strong moon   experienced environmental pliable

88 GENTLE   LENIENT
noble gradual genial   family humble affable

89 FUNCTION   DIGRESS
work deviant immigrate   exodus toil deviate

90 BENEVOLENT
        ridicule compliment
        compliant

MALEVOLENT
defiant hedonism
dilapidated

91 METAPHOR
        pious mystic undevout

SIMILE
irreverent devotee jinx

92 IGNORAMUS
        obfuscation transfer simple

ILLUMINATION
modest scarce encyclopedist

93 DEFICIENT
        modification perfection
        temperance

MODERATE
gluttonous lapse
stigma

94 MALAPROPISM
        solipsism behaviourism
        communism

LINGUISTICS
mathematics psychology
engineering

95 AMORPHOUS
        abundance shower
        harassment

NEBULOUS
torrent profusion
enchantment

Word swap

Underline the two words that must be interchanged to make the following sentences read sensibly. Do not attempt to alter the sentences in any other way.

96 The Health and Safety at Work Act 1976 is securing at aimed your health, safety and welfare.

97 Unlike most typewriters, when you come to the end of a press on a word processor you do not have to line the return key as the word processor brings the cursor to the next line automatically.

98 The equal who gets this job will have a firm commitment to person opportunities.

99 We are a housing London working in north and west association.

100 Holidays grade from 22 to 30 working days annually according to range and length of service.

101 Joyce fell kicking into the chair by the phone, back off her working boots, and went to sleep.

102 Nouns are things words and can name people, creatures, naming and feelings.

103 A subject is a group of sentences that all deal with a single paragraph.

104 In a vault near Paris is kept a small platinum cylinder which serves as the original reference for kilogram standards; copies are sold and made to laboratories worldwide.

105 National Health Service hospital private have contracts under which they are allowed to top up their pay to a limit of 10 per cent with extra earnings from consultants practice.

106 In his conference speech the Prime Minister worried to provide nursery places for every four-year-old; however, privately, the Education Secretary was pledged because her department had estimated each would cost in the region of £1,500 per annum.

107 The National Heritage Secretary began his speech by saying that 'There are at present about 30,000 listed buildings of which slightly under 50,000 are grade 1'.

108 Peter Taylor made a virtue of being impressive and his promotion to Chief Executive within three years of joining the company was widely expected but no less predictable.

109 The 24-year-old grandfather whose lord won a Victoria Cross in the First World War appealed to his fellow peers 'not to let our heads rule our hearts'.

110 Imperial porphyry is an exceptionally ancient stone with royal associations from the hard world because pharaohs and emperors chose it for the material from which to build their tombs.

Sentence sequencing

These questions require you to reorganize four sentences into the order in which they were originally written.

Example:

111 1. As he moved towards the stove he picked up the oven glove.

2. He took care to make sure that the steam would not scald him and he turned off the gas.

3. James looked up from the paper to notice that the kettle was boiling furiously.

4. He poured the water into the teapot successfully.

Answer | 3, 1, 2, 4

Try these:

112 1. Put out your arm when you see the bus coming.

2. Tender the correct change to the conductor.

3. Climb in.

4. Tell the conductor where you want to alight.

Answer

113 1. The engine roared into life.

2. The '57 Chevy careered dangerously into the sunset.

3. There was a stomach-churning grating of the gears.

4. The tyres squealed as it pulled away.

Answer

114 1. The medieval period saw a large growth in the construction of cathedrals.

2. Its main characteristic was parallel stone mullions running the entire height of the windows.

3. One such was perpendicular Gothic.

4. They were built in a number of styles.

Answer

115 1. The carrots cascaded from the scale pan into the bag.

2. The grocer deftly spun it before handing it over.

3. He pulled a paper bag from the hook.

4. Mr Benjamin placed it into his shopping bag.

Answer [   ]

116 1. He proffered a flaring match.

2. 'Have you got a light?' came a once-familiar voice.

3. In its flickering light he recognized her as his former boss.

4. He tentatively asked 'Is your name Karen Moss?'

Answer [   ]

117 1. The former did not reach the South Pole first, but died heroically on his return journey.

2. There were two Antarctic expeditions in 1912.

3. The latter, a Norwegian, was the first man to reach the South Pole, but in comparatively unremarkable circumstances.

4. Arguably, Captain Scott's was more famous than Amundsen's.

Answer [   ]

118 1. Having bought the shares, the stockbroker transferred them to the client.

2. Before the Big Bang in 1986 the method of buying shares in the London market was different.

3. The broker then approached a jobber to buy the shares.

4. The client would approach a stockbroker.

Answer [   ]

119 1. It is so called because being large, slow and buoyant when dead it was the 'right' whale to catch.

2. The decline has been the most pronounced among the larger whales, and scientists fear that a number of species, particularly the right whale, might become extinct.

3. In the 20th century, as fishing methods became more effective, the decline in the whale population occurred very rapidly.

4. Whales are now protected and their numbers are expected to rise.

Answer [   ]

120 1. Frantically he tore at the coils around the neck.

2. Once the bedding was straight, she assured him, 'It's all right, the doctor's on his way.'

3. Gently his mother unravelled the sheet and kissed his fevered brow.

4. The anaconda coiled itself around his body, squeezing the lifeblood from him.

Answer [   ]

121 1. The Institute claims to show that executive pay in the 1980s outstripped that on the factory floor.

2. That Britain's executives are threatening the rate of economic recovery by awarding themselves unwarranted pay rises.

3. The National Institute of Economic and Social Research has apparently confirmed what many have long suspected:

4. What is more, the study found that executive pay rises in the 1990s have little or no connection with company performance.

Answer [   ]

122 1. After the war he served on the cruiser *Jamaica* in the West Indies.

2. The son of a naval engineer, Hugo Janier went to Dartmouth at the age of 13 in 1937.

3. His final post as a captain was in command of the guided-missile destroyer *Bristol*.

4. Graduating during the war, he saw service as a midshipman on the battleship *Rodney*.

Answer [   ]

123 1. The suspect, having been taken to the police station under arrest, as soon as practicable a decision will be made on whether to press charges.

2. In the magistrates' court the case will either be disposed of or adjourned to another sitting.

3. The suspect should be legally arrested by a police officer, designated official or citizen.

4. If charged, the suspect will be detained or released on bail to attend the magistrates' court at a given time on a given day.

Answer [   ]

124 1. Alternatively, on the verdict of guilty, the defendant will be sentenced immediately or have the case adjourned for sentence in order to allow a pre-sentence report to be made.

2. At the end of the speeches the judge will sum up the case for the jury, who will then retire in the custody of the jury bailiff to make their deliberations.

3. Counsel for defence will make her closing speech.

4. Having given their verdict, the defendant, if she is acquitted, is then free to leave.

Answer [   ]

125 1. The disaster was narrowly avoided and the track man received a medal and a reward for his bravery.

2. Imperceptibly at first, the train began to roll down the track, picking up speed.

3. In his eagerness to get clearance from the signalman the train driver climbed down from the cab, forgetting to apply the brakes.

4. Seeing another train on the tracks and the impending disaster, the track worker threw down his shovel, leapt into the cab and applied the brake.

Answer

126 1. Befuddled, she made her way to the door, not knowing who it could be at this hour.

2. Suddenly, Colette was rudely awakened from her dream by an insistent knocking.

3. She had won the national lottery and was about to receive the cheque for £2 million from the television personality Joanna Lumley.

4. Her heart nearly missed a beat when she saw the tall bespectacled man in the leather trench coat outside.

Answer

127 1. This decline is mainly due to a collapse in the 20th century in the price of tin.

2. Tin mining has been a major industry in Cornwall for over 2,500 years.

3. However, there is only one operating tin mine left in Cornwall.

4. In ancient times the Phoenicians traded tin with the Cornish.

Answer

128 1. After all, the person behind you has been a learner too.

2. Don't let the fact that you are the first in the queue influence your judgement about when to go.

3. What you see when you look must decide your action, and nothing else.

4. As a learner you will be conscious of other drivers lining up behind you at junctions.

Answer [   ]

129 1. This was the media response to the Preliminary Report on Homicide.

2. The picture painted by the report itself is more complicated.

3. 'The mentally ill commit one murder a fortnight', proclaimed the headlines.

4. Home Office records suggest that 89 people with probable mental illness committed a murder between 1992 and 1993, more than one a fortnight and 12 per cent of all murders.

Answer [   ]

130 1. Input the relevant data, carry out a spell-check and print the document.

2. Turn on the computer and monitor, key in your password and ensure you have entered the word-processing software.

3. Name and save the file to an appropriate disk and exit the program.

4. Open a document file.

Answer [   ]

131 1. A barrister will then be briefed to present the case in court before a judge.

2. The solicitor may advise that there is a case and write to the opponent's solicitor.

3. The potential litigant must first see a solicitor for preliminary advice.

4. If liability is disputed and cannot otherwise be resolved, pleadings will be issued and a date set for a court hearing.

Answer

132 1. In the re-examination, the witness has the opportunity to rectify any damage done in cross-examination.

2. First, counsel examines his own witness-in-chief to ascertain facts.

3. There are three stages to examining a witness in court.

4. The witness is then made available to the opposition for cross-examination, in which the witness's version of events is explored, clarified or demolished.

Answer

133 1. Unlike many of his school friends who went to university, his family circumstances denied him any chance of higher education.

2. However, he was soon back in Manchester on the staff of the *Evening Chronicle*, before transferring to the rival paper, the *Manchester Evening News*, in a move that was to shape his career.

3. He therefore started to work on the *Blackpool Times* at the age of 17.

4. Educated at Manchester Grammar School, Lord Ardwick reads *The Guardian* every day of his life.

Answer

134 1. He was the prime mover behind the EuroTEC controversial refinancing package, and his resignation was not unexpected.

2. Peter Heitman quit as Chief Executive as EuroTEC completed the final stage of its difficult restructuring plan.

3. It caused the entertainment company's shares to rise 4 pence to 126p.

4. The announcement stated that his replacement was Mr Montgomery, the ambitious and widely respected financial head of Paymore Bank, the principal lender to the troubled corporation.

Answer [   ]

135 1. If you do, dial the number of the extension you want and you will automatically be connected.

2. Alternatively, you must hang on to be dealt with by an operator.

3. On certain telephone switchboards a recorded message will answer your call.

4. It will ask you if you know the extension you want and whether or not you have a touch-tone phone.

Answer [   ]

Five practice tests

Five realistic full-length practice tests follow. Take them as if they were real tests and stick to the time limits. To make them really realistic, set yourself the challenge of trying to better your last score. The level of difficulty of the tests gets progressively higher so you may find you cannot always beat your own score. You will almost certainly be getting better as you practise even if you do not get a higher score each time, because the goalposts are moving.

The tests are intended only as practice timed tests and to serve as an aid to learning, so don't read too much into the results. This sort of practice is a valuable part of your programme of self-study and will help you develop an effective exam technique under realistic conditions and help you further identify your strengths and address any weaknesses.

The later tests include a good number of questions at the level you might expect to get right if you were to obtain a good score in a real graduate test. What I mean by good is a score in the top 25 per cent of candidates. Setting the level of these timed tests is not a fine science, and while they may be appropriate for one candidate, I will not have got it right for others. You will find some hard questions to help you get used to the idea that you will not get them all right and should not spend too long on any one question.

Again remember the most important thing: you have to try really hard to do well in a psychometric test.

Test 1 Practice test of English usage

Over the page you will find 25 questions. In some of the sentences, one of the underlined words or phrases is incorrect in terms of English usage. None has more than one error. If you find the error, choose the appropriate letter. If you find no error, choose the letter D. Place your answer in the box.

Do not turn the page until you are ready to begin. Allow yourself 15 minutes to attempt the questions. Work as quickly as you can.

1
    A   B

<u>Of these</u> dresses, I think this is <u>the prettiest</u>. Do you think this is the

          C   D

more <u>prettier</u>? <u>No error</u>   *Answer*

2
                             A   B   C

Giving the ice cream to my sister and <u>I</u>, <u>my father</u> then got <u>into</u> the car.

    D

<u>No error</u>

                                  Answer

3
                A   B

Of the two dogs <u>that</u> the family <u>owns</u>, the Labrador is the

      C   D

<u>fatter</u>. <u>No error</u>

                                Answer

4
   A   B   C

'<u>To who</u> should I send this letter?' <u>I</u> asked my boss, as I <u>paused</u>

                         D

before his desk. <u>No error</u>

                                Answer

5
   A   B   C

<u>But</u> is it right <u>that</u> these drugs should be <u>proscribed</u>; that is,

                         D

taken out of circulation? <u>No error</u>

                                Answer

6
         A   B

If you <u>were to</u> <u>put fewer</u> than five items in the shopping basket,

           C   D

you <u>could</u> go through the express checkout. <u>No error</u>

                              Answer

7   A   B   C
In comparison <u>with</u> the <u>English</u>, <u>it is always</u> said that the Irish
                          D
are more poetic. <u>No error</u>   *Answer* [   ]

8   A   B
The line <u>managers</u> were advised that they should <u>council</u> their
                          C   D
staff about the impending <u>takeover</u>. <u>No error</u>
                                                  Answer [   ]

9   A
Since I had <u>learnt</u> to love her so much when she was alive, I now
        B   C   D
<u>treasure</u> my <u>mother's-in-law</u> picture. <u>No error</u>
                                                  Answer [   ]

10   A   B   C
The <u>1900s</u> <u>were</u> a time when many <u>Spanish-speaking</u>
                                            D
immigrants arrived in the United States. <u>No error</u>
                                                  Answer [   ]

11   A   B   C
There was scarcely <u>no one</u> in the room <u>to whom</u> I could <u>have</u>
                                    D
entrusted my secret. <u>No error</u>
                                                  Answer [   ]

12   A   B
<u>Taking</u> vitamins is a way of <u>insuring</u> long life, according to the
        C   D
<u>current</u> thinking. <u>No error</u>
                                                  Answer [   ]

13

               A   B

Each of the <u>hotel's</u> 500 rooms <u>were</u> equipped with televisions,

        C   D

baths, <u>kettles</u> and double beds. <u>No error</u>

Answer [＿＿＿＿＿＿]

14

        A   B

<u>To do this gradually</u> must be the <u>best</u> tactic, as to do otherwise

           C   D

would be to <u>jeopardize</u> the project. <u>No error</u>

Answer [＿＿＿＿＿＿]

15

               A   B

<u>Entering the house just before midnight, the broken glass</u> was

                    C D

discovered by my wife and <u>me</u>. <u>No error</u>

Answer [＿＿＿＿＿＿]

16

A   B

'How many <u>gin and tonics</u> would you be able to drink in an

        C   D

evening?' <u>He</u> asked. <u>No error</u>

Answer [＿＿＿＿＿＿]

17

               A

Morphine and other <u>potentially</u> addictive drugs are valuable

        B   C

<u>medically;</u> if abused, however, <u>it</u> can cause untold damage.

     D

<u>No error</u>

Answer [＿＿＿＿＿＿]

18

                                A

According to the village gossip, the <u>local Vicar</u> had to be

    B   C   D

<u>removed </u>from his post for <u>misappropriating</u> funds. <u>No error</u>

Answer

19

                  A   B

We've tried to <u>deliberately stop</u> <u>arguing</u> in front of the children

                  C   D

because we have <u>realized</u> it disturbs them. <u>No error</u>

Answer

20

                                A   B

The following people could be said <u>to have been</u> <u>successful</u>

        C

leaders<u>;</u> Margaret Thatcher, Churchill and Charles de Gaulle.

     D

<u>No error</u>

Answer

21

        A   B

The <u>children's</u> toys were still <u>laying</u> out on the table when the

                  C   D

the parents <u>returned</u>. <u>No error</u>

Answer

22

        A   B

<u>Paula already left</u> by the time <u>I arrived</u>, so I realized that neither

                C   D

she nor <u>I was</u> going to get to the meeting in time. <u>No error</u>

Answer

23
                                       A   B

Every man, woman or child on the ship <u>is</u> able to fit <u>into</u>

                                       C   D

the lifeboat, so no one should fear for <u>his or her</u> life. <u>No error</u>

Answer

24
   A   B   C

<u>Which</u> of these two houses belongs to <u>you</u>? <u>Ours</u> is the house

                      D

on the left. <u>No error</u>

Answer

25
   A   B   C

<u>Us</u> women feel that we have suffered <u>too</u> much at the <u>hands</u>

                     D

of men. <u>No error</u>

Answer

End of test

Reading comprehension and critical reasoning

To answer reading comprehension and critical reading questions you must respond to a series of questions by referring to a passage. The questions require you to comprehend meaning and significance, assess the logic, identify good inference, distinguish a main idea from subordinate ones, single out a correct summary, evaluate interpretations, identify reasonable conclusions, pinpoint the writer's intention or determine the most likely conjectures and hypotheses.

The subjects covered may be drawn from, for example, science, business and current affairs. Typically, questions ask you to identify the key point, supporting points, reasons given, statements the author might agree or disagree with, the best summary of the passage or its conclusions. A series of suggested answers will follow each question and you must select one as correct.

Be careful: if you know something of the subject, you should not bring in information on the subject not contained in the passage. Even if you consider the passage factually incorrect, take the information as given and use it to answer the questions. Be extra careful if it is a subject on which you hold strong views. It is not your task to offer a critique of the passage.

Practice will help you get better at this increasingly common type of test question. You may also need to build your vocabulary. Do this by reading quality daily newspapers and weekly current affairs and scientific journals – lots of them. Get yourself a quality dictionary and thesaurus and discipline yourself to check every word the meaning of which you are unsure.

You will find further practice at this sort of question in another Kogan Page testing series title: *The Graduate Psychometric Test Workbook*.

Test 2 Practice intermediate-level critical reasoning test

In this test there are a total of 29 questions and you are allowed 30 minutes in which to attempt them.

There are two styles of question. In the first, each question makes a statement relating to a passage. It is your task to say whether the statement is necessarily true or false, or whether you cannot tell if it is true or false. You must base your decision only on the information contained in the passage, which you are expected to accept as completely true.

In the second type, each question consists of two statements labelled A and B and there are four possible answers to the questions, namely: both statements are true, both are false, statement A is true while B is false, or B is true while A is false. Your task is to establish which of these situations applies and place your answer in the box or tick the appropriate box.

Do not turn over until you are ready to begin.

Passage 1

To activate the alarm in the computer department you enter the code 1234. The code 2345 provides cover for the print room as well as the computer department. Code 3456 activates the alarm for the whole building, while 4567 covers the sections for accounts and personnel. Staff are only to know the number for the whole building and the department in which they work. In addition to 3456, Scott and Betty have to remember 4567.

1 Scott and Betty work in the same department.

   True   False   Not possible to say

                                          Answer [   ]

2 The maximum number of codes staff have to remember is two.

   True   False   Not possible to say

                                          Answer [   ]

3 The code 2345 provides protection for the print room only.

   True   False   Not possible to say

                                          Answer [   ]

Passage 2

Peter shared a father with Hilary but it is not Steven, the father of John, youngest son of Sylvia (who is Hilary's mother).

4 Sylvia had three children.

   True   False   Not possible to say

                                          Answer [   ]

5 Steven is the father of at least two of Sylvia's children.

   True   False   Not possible to say

                                          Answer

6   Sylvia is Peter's mother.

   True   False   Not possible to say

                                      Answer [   ]

7   John was the offspring of Steven and Sylvia.

   True   False   Not possible to say

                                      Answer [   ]

Passage 3

All scientific statements that are valid state something which is shown by its proof to be so.

8   The passage demonstrates that all valid statements are scientific.

   True   False   Not possible to say

                                      Answer [   ]

9   A valid scientific statement must have proof.

   True   False   Not possible to say

                                      Answer [   ]

10   To be scientific, a statement must be valid.

   True   False   Not possible to say

                                      Answer [   ]

11   A valid scientific statement must state something.

   True   False   Not possible to say

                                      Answer [   ]

Passage 4

The result of subtracting the square of one number from the square of a second gives the same number as is obtained by adding the two numbers, subtracting the first from the second and then multiplying the results of these two calculations.

12   Whatever the values, the same number is obtained.

True   False   Not possible to say

Answer [   ]

13   The first number is the same as the second.

True   False   Not possible to say

Answer [   ]

14   You could divide instead of multiply and get the same answer.

True   False   Not possible to say

Answer [   ]

Passage 5

Nothing can arise out of nothing and matter cannot vanish, but only be altered to take another form.

15   If you weigh something, burn it, then weigh it again, the difference is the weight of the smoke.

True   False   Not possible to say

Answer [   ]

16   There is a finite amount of matter in the universe.

True   False   Not possible to say

Answer [   ]

17   It is impossible for the amount of diamonds in the universe to decrease.

   True   False   Not possible to say

                                          Answer [   ]

18   The amount of matter in the universe will neither increase nor decrease.

   True   False   Not possible to say

                                          Answer [   ]

19   It should be possible to achieve the alchemists' dream of turning base metals into gold.

   True   False   Not possible to say

                                          Answer [   ]

Passage 6

Mrs Brewer, the office manager, was charged with responsibility for replacing the existing photocopier. The specifications were to remain the same in that the machine was to be able to make 50,000 copies a month, operate at least at 40 copies a minute and have the facility for double-sided copying, a feed tray and a sorter bin. She was told that she could consider ex-demonstration or new machines but must not purchase a service agreement.

   Mrs Brewer embarked on the task with some apprehension, as she was well aware of the bad reputation of photocopier sales staff. She decided to write out a list of specifications and sent this to a number of companies requesting written quotations and details of their products. Soon afterwards, she started to receive calls from the company representatives offering her all kinds of deals.

20   Statement: A   Mrs Brewer requested that the sales representatives telephone her.

                    B   She wanted a machine that could handle double-sided copying.

   A Correct   A Correct   A Incorrect   A Incorrect
   B Correct   B Incorrect   B Correct   B Incorrect

   [   ]   [   ]   [   ]   [   ]

21 Statement: A A service agreement was to be part of the deal.

B More features were required of the new machine.

A Correct	A Correct	A Incorrect	A Incorrect
B Correct	B Incorrect	B Correct	B Incorrect
☐	☐	☐	☐

22 Statement: A Mrs Brewer requires the sales representatives to send her two types of information.

B She has a preference for a new machine rather than one that has been reconditioned.

A Correct	A Correct	A Incorrect	A Incorrect
B Correct	B Incorrect	B Correct	B Incorrect
☐	☐	☐	☐

23 Statement: A While she was apprehensive, Mrs Brewer was able to take some consolation from the fact that she was not solely responsible for the decision over which copier to purchase.

B Photocopier sales staff have a reputation.

A Correct	A Correct	A Incorrect	A Incorrect
B Correct	B Incorrect	B Correct	B Incorrect
☐	☐	☐	☐

24 Statement: A Mrs Brewer's copier would need to undertake over half a million copies a year.

B A machine that could undertake just under 2,000 copies an hour would not meet her specification.

A Correct	A Correct	A Incorrect	A Incorrect
B Correct	B Incorrect	B Correct	B Incorrect
☐	☐	☐	☐

Passage 7

Mr Waters, a tool-maker with Johnson & Matthew, left his machine to record in the company's accident book the fact that he had received a small splinter of steel in his thumb. This was a common accident for someone in his trade and he knew the company nurse would have to remove it, otherwise it was likely to become infected.

As he wrote down the circumstances of his accident he noticed a leaflet which read: 'The Health and Safety at Work Act is aimed at securing the health, safety and welfare of all workers. It requires employers to ensure the safety of their employees at work but also places a legal responsibility on every individual, whilst at work, to take care of their own and their colleagues' health and safety. Workers must cooperate with their employers to ensure that their place of work is safe. The Act allows that both employers and employees can be fined or sent to prison if they fail to fulfil their legal duties. In large organizations health and safety representatives are elected to represent the workers and to carry out safety checks.'

25 Statement: A The Act requires every individual to take care to avoid injury to themselves.
           B Mr Waters has a legal duty to consider the safety of his fellow workers.

A Correct	A Correct	A Incorrect	A Incorrect
B Correct	B Incorrect	B Correct	B Incorrect
☐	☐	☐	☐

26 Statement: A The Act requires all employers to have safety representatives.
           B Mr Waters read that he would receive compensation for his injury.

A Correct	A Correct	A Incorrect	A Incorrect
B Correct	B Incorrect	B Correct	B Incorrect
☐	☐	☐	☐

27 Statement: A Mr Waters' employers risk imprisonment or a fine if
              they do not maintain a safe place of work.
           B Mr Waters' thumb required medical attention.

A Correct	A Correct	A Incorrect	A Incorrect
B Correct	B Incorrect	B Correct	B Incorrect

28 Statement: A Mr Waters is required to record the circumstances of
              the accident in the accident book.
           B Fortunately, the book was kept beside Mr Waters'
              machine.

A Correct	A Correct	A Incorrect	A Incorrect
B Correct	B Incorrect	B Correct	B Incorrect

29 Statement: A The company provided a written explanation of the
              Health and Safety at Work Act.
           B Splinters of metal were an occupational hazard for
              tool-makers.

A Correct	A Correct	A Incorrect	A Incorrect
B Correct	B Incorrect	B Correct	B Incorrect

End of test

Test 3 Practice intermediate-level critical reasoning test

Over the page you will find a test comprising 36 questions. Complete the test in 25 minutes.

Your task is to decide from the information presented in a passage or flow diagram whether or not the statements or questions that follow are true or false, or that you cannot tell.

Do not turn the page until you are ready to begin.

Passage 1

Research suggests that a sustained increase in spending on infrastructure is associated with an increase in macroeconomic growth, albeit not as convincingly in the data as intuition would suggest.

Question 1

High levels of investment spent on infrastructure are fairly well correlated with economic growth.

    True   False   Cannot tell   *Answer*

Question 2

High spending tends to promote productivity gains and faster economic growth.

    True   False   Cannot tell   *Answer*

Question 3

Building a new rail link might be beneficial to macro growth.

    True   False   Cannot tell   *Answer*

Passage 2

Quarter 3, 1999 data showed that the US economy expanded by just 0.4 per cent against a 1.1 per cent rise in the first quarter of 1999. All that year, forecasters argued that the US dollar was overvalued, yet it continued to appreciate against every other currency. Finally, in the third quarter the dollar weakened.

Question 4

US economic growth cooled markedly during 1999.

    True   False   Cannot tell   *Answer*

Question 5

Depreciation of the US currency could easily gather momentum during the remainder of 1999.

    True   False   Cannot tell   *Answer*

Question 6

Economic growth was a factor behind the appreciation of the US dollar.

True   False   Cannot tell   *Answer* [   ]

Question 7

An American coming to Europe in the autumn of 1999 found he could buy more with his dollars than when he visited Europe earlier that year.

True   False   Cannot tell   *Answer* [   ]

Passage 3

In a survey, companies' total cash-flow position was found to have worsened slightly; 22 per cent reported cash-flow problems, compared with 19 per cent in the previous survey. However, this result is still well below the trend average of 29 per cent over the life of the survey.

Question 8

This still is a pretty impressive result.

True   False   Cannot tell   *Answer* [   ]

Question 9

The survey suggests that the respondents' cash-flow management has improved over the life of the survey.

True   False   Cannot tell   *Answer* [   ]

Question 10

Late payment remains the main source of cash-flow problems for respondents.

True   False   Cannot tell   *Answer* [   ]

Passage 4

Data show that two-thirds of companies surveyed advertised on the internet, compared with just half of companies surveyed 18 months ago.

Question 11
The number of companies advertising on the internet has increased markedly.

True   False   Cannot tell   *Answer* [   ]

Question 12
In terms of its impact on company performance and possibly also in terms of its implications for the wider economy, the survey suggests that internet use has not yet reached its full potential.

True   False   Cannot tell   *Answer* [   ]

Passage 5
Sixteen per cent of firms report using the internet in central purchasing, of which almost 43 per cent report making slight cost savings, 5 per cent report making significant savings, 28 per cent suggest that it is too early to tell whether or not savings are being made, while the remaining respondents said that no savings were being made.

Question 13
It is fair to conclude that, for some respondents, use of the internet has resulted in a reduction in the cost of central purchases.

True   False   Cannot tell   *Answer* [   ]

Question 14
The majority of respondents who used the internet for central purchasing either saw no cost benefit or reported that it was too early to tell.

True   False   Cannot tell   *Answer* [   ]

Question 15
The majority of respondents used the internet for central purchases.

True   False   Cannot tell   *Answer* [   ]

Passage 6
Sales performance varies by industrial sector in terms of sales and orders: retailing performed least well and business and other services performed best. Industries with above sector-average sales include construction,

wholesale, and hotel and catering. While manufacturing sales remain below the industrial sector-average, sales have improved for this and the last three years.

Question 16
Business and other services outperform other sectors in sales and orders.

     True   False   Cannot tell   *Answer*   [   ]

Question 17
Manufacturing continues to pick up.

     True   False   Cannot tell   *Answer*   [   ]

Question 18
Considerable price pressures exist in retailing.

     True   False   Cannot tell   *Answer*   [   ]

Question 19
Transport and communication and hotel and catering were the only sectors reporting above sector-average sales.

     True   False   Cannot tell   *Answer*   [   ]

Question 20
The sector 'Business and Other Services' included wholesale.

     True   False   Cannot tell   *Answer*   [   ]

Passage 7

Net export balance sharply rose to 16 per cent following net balances of 4 per cent each in the previous two surveys; 41 per cent of companies reported higher export orders, against 25 per cent reporting lower export orders, compared with levels of 33 per cent and 29 per cent six months ago.

Question 21
More companies report lower export orders than six months ago.

     True   False   Cannot tell   *Answer*   [   ]

Question 22
All companies are expanding sales of goods and services abroad.

True   False   Cannot tell   *Answer*   [   ]

Question 23
More companies have reported higher export orders.

True   False   Cannot tell   *Answer*   [   ]

Question 24
Export orders show surprise growth.

True   False   Cannot tell   *Answer*   [   ]

Passage 8

Companies surveyed reported a negative net price balance of 3 per cent in the second half of 2000. Nineteen per cent of firms reported raising prices, while 22 per cent reported cutting prices. This result extends the period of price cuts to three years.

Question 25
All companies are lowering the prices that they charge their customers.

True   False   Cannot tell   *Answer*   [   ]

Question 26
Falling prices are squeezing profits.

True   False   Cannot tell   *Answer*   [   ]

Question 27
The period of price cutting continued into the second half of 2000.

True   False   Cannot tell   *Answer*   [   ]

Question 28
It is no coincidence that the percentage difference between firms that report raising prices and those cutting prices is the same as the second half percentage figure for negative net price balance.

True   False   Cannot tell   *Answer*   [   ]

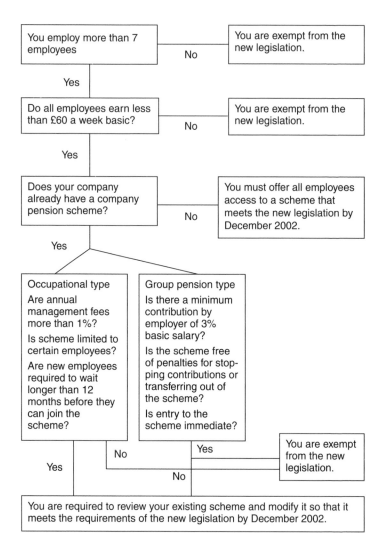

FIGURE 10 Action an employer must take following new government legislation on employee pensions

Questions

29   You employ six employees and currently offer an occupational-type scheme that has a management fee each year of 1 per cent.

No action required
Action required
Not enough information provided to decide

Answer _____

30   Your current occupational scheme is not offered to full-time employees.

No action required
Action required
Not enough information provided to decide

Answer _____

31   Your company has a group pension scheme. Directors of the company receive a contribution of 10 per cent of basic salary after three months' service. All staff receive a minimum employer contribution of 3 per cent. The scheme is free of penalties and all staff may join immediately.

No action required
Action required
Not enough information provided to decide

Answer _____

32   Nine out of 13 of your employees earn less than the legislationally exempt minimum salary.

No action required
Action required
Not enough information provided to decide

Answer _____

33 Entry to your occupational scheme is offered to all employees. There is no annual management fee and employees wait 10 months to join.

No action required
Action required
Not enough information provided to decide

Answer

34 Your company already has a pension scheme that allows new employees to join immediately and has no penalties for stopping or starting.

No action required
Action required
Not enough information provided to decide

Answer

35 You offer a group pension scheme for all employees after three months' service with no exit penalties.

No action required
Action required
Not enough information provided to decide

Answer

36 A member of staff declines to join your company complaint scheme.

No action required
Action required
Not enough information provided to decide

Answer

End of test

Test 4 Practice advanced-level reading comprehension and critical reasoning test

Over the page you will find 23 questions relating to five passages. Allow yourself 25 minutes to complete the test. Do not turn the page until you are ready to begin.

In this test you are presented with a series of short passages each followed by three, four or sometimes five statements or questions relating to them. Your task is to pick one of the suggested responses as the correct one to the statement or question.

Be especially careful if you know lots about the subject covered by a passage as you are then more likely to involve your personal knowledge or opinions and as a result risk getting the question wrong!

In the real tests you have very little time to read the passage and answer the questions.

Do not make the mistake of not practising if you find these questions easy when you are free of the pressure of time. In the real test you will only have time for one careful reading. You will have to switch really fast between vastly different subject matter with each passage and keep up a very high level of concentration right to the end. This all takes practice to get really good at.

Do not turn the page until you are ready to begin.

Passage 1

A paper plane should be made by folding a single sheet of A4 paper and not involve any cuts or the addition of anything such as sticky tape, glue or weights. The indoor flight record for such a plane is over 60 metres. The aerodynamics involved are as complex as the principles behind any plane but the secret to one built from paper is ease of construction, folds that impart strength, the correct location of the centre of balance, minimum drag and maximum lift. The best designs seem to involve a blunt nose made from multiple folds. This makes the craft strongest at the point of impact in the hopefully many crash landings. It also sets the centre of gravity further back than on a pointed nose design and so affords more stable flight. The wing shape that affords the longest flights is delta, cambered upwards to increase lift by forcing the air as it passes over the wind through a greater angle. A plane with such wings is capable of flight in excess of 20 seconds when launched from a height of 2 metres in still air.

Question 1

The nose and wing shape are not key to the design of a successful paper plane.

True   False   Cannot tell   *Answer* [   ]

Question 2

Outside, where wind conditions and thermal lifts may be harnessed, flights may last considerably longer and go much further than 60 metres.

True   False   Cannot tell   *Answer* [   ]

Question 3

The point that wings should be slightly convex so that they increase lift is made in the passage.

True   False   Cannot tell   *Answer* [   ]

Question 4

The case made in the passage would be greatly weakened if a paper plane were made using cuts, glue and weights.

True   False   Cannot tell   *Answer* [   ]

Passage 2

We may not much like the fact but we are 99.9 per cent identical. This is because 99.9 per cent of our DNA is common to every person, and the Human Genome Project is rightly celebrated for sequencing it. But what of the remaining 0.1 per cent? It is far more significant than one might assume, because if it were not for this minute percentage, there would be no individual differences. We would be clones. These variations in the human code account for all individual idiosyncrasies. They are responsible for the differences between ethnic and racial groups. Perhaps most interesting of all, they also explain why some of us enjoy good health while others are more susceptible to many common diseases. It is thought that the mapping of the remaining 0.1 per cent of human DNA will hasten the identity of new ways to treat common ailments such as obesity, cancer and heart disease. The work will prove particularly useful in the search for new diagnostic tests, the customizing of treatments to best suit an individual's genetic code and, ultimately, the development of new drugs that target the DNA linked to a particular disease. The task of charting the inherited differences in the human genome has fallen to 200 scientists drawn from nine countries across every populated continent.

Question 5

Sequencing is mentioned in the passage in relation to the work of the Human Genome Project.

    True   False   Cannot tell   *Answer* [＿＿＿＿＿＿＿]

Question 6

The scientists responsible for charting inherited differences in the human genome will screen people drawn from every populated continent.

    True   False   Cannot tell   *Answer* [＿＿＿＿＿＿＿]

Question 7

The conclusion that some of us enjoy good health while others are more susceptible to many common diseases relies on the premise that we are 99.9 per cent genetically identical.

    True   False   Cannot tell   *Answer* [＿＿＿＿＿＿＿]

Question 8

It can be inferred from the passage that the work will speed up the development of new treatments.

True   False   Cannot tell   *Answer* [   ]

Passage 3

He that is nourished by the acorns that he picked up under an oak, or the apples he gathered from the trees in the wood, has certainly appropriated them to himself. Nobody can deny but the nourishment is his. I ask, then, when did they begin to be his? when he digested? or when he ate? or when he boiled? or when he brought them home? or when he picked them up? And it is plain, if the first gathering made them not his, nothing else could. That labour put a distinction between them and common. That added something to them more than Nature, the common mother of all, and so they became his private right...

His labour hath taken it out of the hands of Nature where it was common, and belonged equally to all her children, and hath thereby appropriated it to himself...

It will, perhaps, be objected to this, that if gathering the acorns or other fruits of the earth, etc, makes a right to them, then anybody may engross as much as he will. To which I answer, Not so. The same law of Nature that does by this means give us property, does also bound that property too. 'God had given us all things richly.' Is the voice of reason confirmed by inspiration? But how far has He given it us – 'to enjoy'? As much as anyone can make use of to advantage of life before it spoils, so much he may by his labour fix a property in. Whatever is beyond this is more than his share, and belongs to others...

He who gathered as much of the wild fruit, killed, caught, or tamed as many of the beasts as he could – he that so employed his pains about any of the spontaneous products of Nature as any way to alter them from the state Nature put them in, by placing any of his labour on them, did thereby acquire a property in them, but if they perished in his possession without their due use – if the fruits rotted or the venison putrefied before he could spend it, he offended against the common law of Nature, and was liable to be punished:

he invaded his neighbour's share, for he had no right farther than his use called for any of them, and they might serve to afford him conveniences of life.

John Locke, Section V, *An Essay Concerning the True Original, Extent, and End of Civil Government* (1690)

Question 9
The primary purpose of this passage is to:

A   Describe the way in which we lived before civilization

B   Promote the equal sharing of the world's scarce resources

C   Investigate the basis for legitimate private property

D   None of these   *Answer*

Question 10
The objection that Locke's argument allows one to 'engross as much as he will' fails because:

A   God has given us all things richly so we can take as much as we like

B   The fruit will rot and the venison will putrefy, so there is no point taking more than you need

C   The law of Nature dictates that if we take more than we can use, we have taken something that belongs to others

D   None of these   *Answer*

Question 11
Which of the following words describe the tone of the passage?

A   Humorous

B   Contrived

C   Journalistic

D   None of these   *Answer*

Question 12

Locke suggests that it is unequivocal that we have appropriated something for ourselves if we:

A   Collected it and carried it away

B   Have eaten and digested it

C   Stored it for winter

D   None of these   *Answer*   [   ]

Question 13

In the passage Locke argues that you can acquire something as your own property if you:

A   Share it with others

B   Inherit it

C   Seize a neighbour's share

D   None of these   *Answer*   [   ]

Passage 4

The produce of labour constitutes the natural recompense or wages of labour.

In that original state of things, which precedes both the appropriation of land and the accumulation of stock, the whole produce of labour belongs to the labourer. He has neither landlord nor master to share with him.

Had this state continued, the wages of labour would have augmented with all those improvements in its productive powers, to which the division of labour gives occasion. All things would gradually have become cheaper. They would have been produced by a smaller quantity of labour; and as the commodities produced by equal quantities of labour would naturally in this state of things be exchanged for one another, they would have been purchased likewise with the produce of a small quantity.

But though all things would have become cheaper in reality, in appearance many things might have become dearer than before, or have been exchanged for a greater quantity of other goods. Let us suppose, for example, that in the greater part of employments the productive powers of labour had been improved tenfold, or that a day's labour could produce only ten times the quantity of work which it had done originally, but that in a particular employ-ment they had been improved only to double, or that a day's labour could produce only twice the quantity of work which it had done before. In exchang-ing the produce of a day's labour in the greater part of employments, for that of a day's labour in this particular one, ten times the original quantity of work in them would purchase only twice the original quantity in it. Any particular quantity in it, therefore, a pound weight, for example, would appear to be five times dearer than before. In reality, however, it would be twice as cheap. Though it required five times the quantity of other goods to purchase it, it would require only half the quantity of labour either to purchase or to produce it. The acquisition, therefore, would be twice as easy as before.

Adam Smith, Of the Wages of Labour, Chapter VIII, Volume 1, *The Wealth of Nations* (1776)

Question 14
The passage addresses which of the following issues?

A   The effect of division of labour on productive power

B   The effect on prices if labourers were to keep all the product of their labour

C   The effect on prices if labourers kept all the product of their labour and their labour benefited from improvements in productive power.

D   None of these

Answer [   ]

Question 15
If labourers were to keep all the product of their labour, Smith states things would become cheaper in:

A   Reality

B   Appearance

C   The marketplace

D   None of these

Answer [   ]

Question 16

If the productive power of labour is improved tenfold, Smith claimed that:

A   Things would appear five times cheaper

B   Things would in reality be twice as cheap

C   Things would appear five times dearer

D   None of these

Answer   _____

Question 17

Smith holds that commodities would continue to be exchanged in equal quantities only if:

A   One product benefited more from improvements in productive power than the other

B   Labour was divided, land appropriated and stock accumulated

C   Both products benefited equally from improvements in productive power

D   None of these   *Answer*   _____

Question 18

According to Smith, while in reality things would become cheaper, in appearance:

A   All things would become dearer

B   Some things would become dearer

C   Some things might become dearer

D   None of these   *Answer*   _____

Passage 5

Now suppose that the average amount of the daily necessaries of a labouring man require six hours of average labour for their production. Suppose, moreover, six hours of average labour to be also realised in a quantity of gold equal to three shillings. Then three shillings would be the Price, or the monetary expression of the Daily Value of that man's Labouring Power. If he worked daily six hours he would daily produce a value sufficient to buy the average amount of his daily necessaries, or to maintain himself as a labouring man.

But our man is a wages labourer. He must, therefore, sell his labouring power to a capitalist. If he sells it at three shillings daily, or 18 shillings weekly, he sells it at its value. Suppose him to be a spinner. If he works six hours daily he will add to the cotton a value of three shillings daily. This value, daily added by him, would be the exact equivalent for the wages, or the price of his labouring power, received daily. But in that case no surplus value or surplus produce whatever would go to the capitalist. Here, then, we come to the rub...

The value of the labouring power is determined by the quantity of labour necessary to maintain or reproduce it, but the use of that labouring power is only limited by the active energies and the physical strength of the labourer... Take the example of our spinner. We have seen that, to daily reproduce his labouring power, he must daily reproduce a value of three shillings, which he will do by working six hours daily. But this does not disable him from working ten or twelve or more hours a day. But by paying the daily or weekly value of the spinner's labouring power, the capitalist has acquired the right of using the labouring power during the whole day or week. He will, therefore, make him work, say, daily for twelve hours. Over and above the six hours required to replace his wages, or the value of his labouring power, he will, therefore, have to work six other hours, which I shall call surplus labour, which surplus labour will realise itself in a surplus value and a surplus produce. If our spinner, for example, by his daily labour of six hours, added three shillings' value to the cotton, a value forming an exact equivalent to his wages, he will, in twelve hours, add six shillings' worth to the cotton, and produce a proportional surplus of yarn. As he has sold his labouring power to the capitalist, the whole value or produce created by him belongs to the capitalist, the owner... of his labouring power.

Karl Marx, Production of Surplus Value, Section VIII, *Wages, Price and Profit* (1865)

Question 19
Marx holds that 'the rub' is:

A   That the spinner sells his labouring power at its value

B   That the spinner works a 12-hour day

C   That the spinner's surplus value goes to the capitalist

D   None of these

Answer

Question 20
With which of the following ideas would the author probably agree?

A   Industrial profit is a legitimate part of the value of the commodity

B   Industrial profit is only a different name for the unpaid labour enclosed in a commodity

C   If wages fall, profits fall; if wages rise, profits will rise

D   None of these

Answer

Question 21
Identify from the following a correct restatement of the main idea of the passage:

A   The amount of surplus value depends on the ratio in which the working day is prolonged over the time it takes for the working man to replace his wages

B   A general rise in the rate of wages would result in a fall in the general rate of profit

C   It is the constant tendency of capitalists to stretch the working day to its utmost physically possible length

D   None of these

Answer

Question 22

Which of the following statements best describes the approach taken by Marx in the passage?

A   He refutes a stated view

B   He sets out to be expansive

C   His objective is to compare and contrast

D   None of these

Answer

Question 23

According to Marx, the spinner's daily necessities require:

A   Three shillings

B   Six hours of average labour

C   A 12-hour working day

D   None of these

Answer

End of test

Test 5 Practice advanced-level reading comprehension and critical reasoning test

This test comprises 30 questions and you are allowed 30 minutes in which to attempt them.

In this test you are presented with a series of short passages each followed by three, four or sometimes five statements or questions relating to them. Your task is to indicate whether the statement or question is true or false, or you cannot tell.

With this type of question you sometimes find yourself saying something is true or false that you know not to be the case or confirming as true or false something with which you do not personally agree. This is because you rely only on the content of the passage to answer the questions. Be especially careful if you know lots about the subject covered by a passage as you are then more likely to involve your personal knowledge or opinions and as a result risk getting the question wrong!

In the real tests you have very little time to read the passage and answer the questions.

Do not make the mistake of not practising if you find these questions easy when you are free of the pressure of time. In the real test you will only have time for one careful reading. You will have to switch really fast between vastly different subject matter with each passage and keep up a very high level of concentration right to the end. This all takes practice to get really good at.

This question type has become very popular in recent years and features in many graduate and management psychometric tests. With practice you can show a considerable improvement in your score.

Do not turn the page until you are ready to begin.

Passage 1

European road congestion is forecast to grow by 70 per cent by 2010 and the total distance travelled by rail is expected to increase 60 per cent by 2024. Despite the obvious increase in demand for space on our roads and trains, governments are failing to match forecast growth with investment in either mode of transport. In the 10 worst areas the problems are already chronic, with immediate investment needed if sufficient capacity is to be created to cope even with current demand. New roads and tracks, and longer platforms that can handle longer trains, are already needed to relieve bottlenecks, congestion and severe overcrowding, especially during peak hours. Despite demand, there are no plans to significantly expand road and rail networks, and indeed closures and cuts in funding are on the agenda in a number of member states. There are considerable doubts that those few projects that are currently supported by governments will ever be completed because ministers are refusing to say how much public money they will receive.

Q1 You can infer from the passage that people are giving up their cars to undertake journeys by train.

   True   False   Cannot tell   *Answer* [   ]

Q2 Train users in Europe face a future of overcrowded networks, higher fares, slower journey times and in some states closures.

   True   False   Cannot tell   *Answer* [   ]

Q3 The latter half of the passage is taken up with the issue of the diminutive public investment in the expansion of the railways.

   True   False   Cannot tell   *Answer* [   ]

Q4 In the worst 10 areas immediate investment is already needed because during peak periods they suffer bottlenecks, congestion and severe overcrowding.

   True   False   Cannot tell   *Answer* [   ]

Q5   From a reading of the passage it is hard to arrive at any other conclusion but that at home European travellers face a bleak future of overcrowding and congestion.

True   False   Cannot tell   *Answer* [   ]

Passage 2

Recent research has provided further stark evidence of the educational apartheid dividing the achievements of bright children from low- and high-income families. The study followed for many years the progress of a sample of almost 40,000 of the brightest children. Two-thirds were drawn from low-income families. The research found that almost all the able children from high-income families realized three or more A grades in exams at the age of 18 years. But it was found that only 1 in 4 of the most able children from low-income families achieved similar grades. The effect of this inequality puts the low-income, bright child at a considerable disadvantage. A bright child from a high-income family was found to have a 1 in 2 chance of gaining a place at one of the best universities. A bright child from a low-income family had only a 1 in 10 chance of gaining such a place. The bright children from high-income families were themselves very likely to enjoy a high income in their working life. A significant majority of the bright children from low-income families failed to earn above the national average wage.

Q6   The statement that 'bright children from poor homes are failing to get the same grades as their rich counterparts' expresses the main theme of the passage.

True   False   Cannot tell   *Answer* [   ]

Q7   The primary objective of the passage was to report the findings and the reaction to the recent research.

True   False   Cannot tell   *Answer* [   ]

Q8   It is stated in the passage that the divide in the educational achievement of rich and poor children was already known about.

True   False   Cannot tell   *Answer* [   ]

Q9 You can rightly describe the tone of the passage as either anecdotal or dogmatic.

True   False   Cannot tell   *Answer* [ ]

Q10 It can be inferred from the passage that a child needs parental encouragement and resources such as a quiet place to study to realize his or her educational potential.

True   False   Cannot tell   *Answer* [ ]

Passage 3

Until recently almost everything we knew about the giant squid was deduced from dead specimens washed up on beaches or found in the stomachs of whales. Very occasionally there were sightings and even reported attacks on boats. The largest specimens are believed to reach almost 18 metres. A Japanese team decided to use sperm whale migration patterns to try to locate and film the squid in their natural habitat. They made up a fishing line and baited it with hooks and fish. On the line they also hung lights and a camera and they lowered it a kilometre into the ocean at a location well known for sightings of sperm whales. They reasoned that where sperm whales congregate might be a good place to film the squid. Their plan worked. When they recovered their line and examined the film they watched shoot out from the dark a giant squid with tentacles outstretched and a snapping beak to attack one of the bated hooks. The squid became caught and struggled furiously until it was able to free itself. The team believe their film is the first ever of a giant squid alive in its natural habitat. They hope that careful study of the footage will reveal much new information about the behaviour of this elusive creature.

Q11 The observed giant squid was 18 metres in length.

True   False   Cannot tell   *Answer* [ ]

Q12 It can be inferred from that passage that the researchers reasoned that where the whales congregate might be a good place to film the squid.

True   False   Cannot tell   *Answer* [ ]

Q13 The researchers will be able to conjecture that the giant squid is a vigorous hunter.

True   False   Cannot tell   *Answer*   [   ]

Q14 It can be deduced from the passage that giant squid ordinarily live at depths of 1,000 metres.

True   False   Cannot tell   *Answer*   [   ]

Q15 Where sperm whales congregate is a good place to film giant squid because sperm whales eat them.

True   False   Cannot tell   *Answer*   [   ]

Passage 4

We all know that our criminal system is failing but how many of us know the extent of the failure? Do you know, for example, that nine out of ten offenders reoffend within two years of completing their punishment? No wonder that our prisons are so overcrowded that programmes of education and rehabilitation have been abandoned. Staff simply do not have the time or resources to run them any longer. An offender rarely gets a prison sentence on the occasion of their first conviction. They are far more likely to be sentenced to a curfew monitored by an electronic tag and police surveillance. Many do not even wait for the end of their period of curfew before they reoffend. Large numbers breach their curfew repeatedly and even remove their electronic tags. But by the time they have appeared before the judge on the third or fourth occasion, all hope that community-based punishments will work is abandoned and the persistent offender is sentenced to a period of imprisonment.

Q16 The main claim of the passage is that our criminal system is failing to prevent reoffending.

True   False   Cannot tell   *Answer*   [   ]

Q17 You can infer from the passage that the author believes that a major objective of punishment is to deter reoffending.

True   False   Cannot tell   *Answer*   [   ]

Q18 Under the current system even the fear of being caught and punished again is failing to deter.

True   False   Cannot tell   *Answer* [   ]

Q19 Rehabilitation programmes have been abandoned because they do not prevent reoffending.

True   False   Cannot tell   *Answer* [   ]

Q20 From the passage it is clear that we need to find alternative workable solutions to tackle this very real challenge to society.

True   False   Cannot tell   *Answer* [   ]

Passage 5

Colorectal cancer occurs in the colon or rectum. It is more common among men than women and the majority of cases occur in the over-50s. Triggers are thought to be little or no exercise and excessive weight. A propensity for the disease is also known to be inherited. Diet is believed to play an important role both in the risk of developing the disease and in its prevention. It used to be thought that a diet high in fibre greatly reduced the risk of colorectal cancer; however, it is now thought that eating too much red meat and milk products has a much stronger, unfortunately, negative association and increases the risk of the disease notably. It so happens that people with high-fibre diets eat less red meat and milk products than people with low-fibre diets. People who eat lots of fibre also tend to enjoy a lifestyle with many other factors that may confer a lower risk of contracting colorectal cancer. If there is any accepted truism regarding diet, lifestyle and the risk of contacting colorectal cancer, it is that it is no longer the view that eating lots of fibre has an inverse association. Today dietitians are likely to stress the factors that give rise to greater risk, and top of the list of factor will be the consumption of too much alcohol.

Q21 The author would agree that there is no adverse association between colorectal cancer and a diet rich in fibre.

True   False   Cannot tell   *Answer* [   ]

Q22   A diet of cereals, vegetables and fruit does protect against diseases such as heart disease.

True   False   Cannot tell   *Answer*   [   ]

Q23   It is not coincidental that people who eat a diet rich in fibre such as whole grains, fruit and vegetables are less likely to get colorectal cancer then people with a diet poor in fibre.

True   False   Cannot tell   *Answer*   [   ]

Q24   When cancer of the colon occurs, a family history of the disease may be found.

True   False   Cannot tell   *Answer*   [   ]

Q25   The author would agree that an inverse association exists between eating lots of fibre and rates of colon cancer.

True   False   Cannot tell   *Answer*   [   ]

Passage 6

Nuclear power generation is being reconsidered because so many industrialized countries are failing to reduce the level of their carbon emissions through energy efficiencies or renewable power. Some advisers therefore feel that the industrialized world has no alternative but to return to nuclear power, at least until renewable alternatives become available. Nuclear power, which can generate electricity without emitting CO_2, is seen as a necessary evil that can help governments meet future and seemingly ever-increasing demand for more power without increasing the level of carbon emissions.

Proposals to look to nuclear power as a means to address global warming have not been welcomed by all environmental scientists and campaigners. Many argue that nuclear power is far from clean and at some stages of its life cycle, for example when the uranium is mined and refined, is not carbon free. They raise the well-known objections to nuclear power of waste storage, the risk of radioactive leaks, the threat of terrorism, the cost of decommissioning and the risk of the spread of nuclear weapons.

Q26 The statement that nuclear power is far from clean and at some stages of its life cycle, for example when the uranium is mined and refined, is not carbon free is made in support of the main theme of the passage.

True   False   Cannot tell   *Answer* ☐

Q27 If viable renewable sources of energy were available now, then the case made in the passage for nuclear would be greatly weakened.

True   False   Cannot tell   *Answer* ☐

Q28 The claims that nuclear power can generate electricity without emitting CO_2 and that nuclear power is far from clean at some stages of its life cycle are contradictory.

True   False   Cannot tell   *Answer* ☐

Q29 The long-term answer to global warming lies not in nuclear but in greater efforts and investment in renewable wind, wave and tidal power sources and in more energy efficiency.

True   False   Cannot tell   *Answer* ☐

Q30 It is stated in the passage that nuclear power can help to reduce green-house emissions.

True   False   Cannot tell   *Answer* ☐

End of test

Interpretation of your score

A score of 23 or higher

This is the only score that you should be content with if you face a verbal test and are applying for a graduate position on sought-after graduate management programmes or traineeships. From my experience, a score over 23 should see you through to the next stage in the recruitment process, but this will vary from campaign to campaign and, like most things, is not a certainty.

A score between 16 and 22

This is a very wide category of score and will include the near-miss candidate as well as someone who did only moderately well. So, decide where you believe you are on this scale and set about a systematic programme of practice in order to improve your score. Be prepared to undertake a lot of practice if your score was at the lower end of the scale.

A score below 15

Employers are increasingly looking for all-round candidates and will be looking for candidates who realize well-balanced scores across all the tests. Reflect on the reason for your score. Did you spend too long on questions and so run out of time before you could attempt sufficient questions? Do you need to improve your accuracy when working quickly under the pressure of an exam? Once you have settled on the cause, set about a programme of revision under realistic practice conditions. Above all else, do not give up. Keep working and you will witness a marked improvement in your performance in these very common tests.

CHAPTER 5

Answers and many explanations

Chapter 2

Practice at 40 more personality questionnaire statements

S1 *Explanation:* Perhaps we all do let small things upset us more than they should, but not usually in work, and remember that this is the context of these questions, so you should almost certainly have disagreed with this statement.

S2 *Explanation:* Every employer will have some regulations and procedures and it will be reasonable to expect you to follow them. Employers therefore will most likely expect agreement with this statement.

S3 *Explanation:* This is a statement with which you should not agree as it implies that you will not work as soon as your boss turns their back.

S4 *Explanation:* Agreement implies a reactive approach and risks an employer concluding that you see little merit in a proactive style of working where you might for example attempt to design and deploy strategies in anticipation of likely events.

S5 *Explanation:* You almost certainly should agree if you want to work in a fast-moving, competitive environment.

S6 *Explanation:* Agreement with this statement would risk the interpretation that you were not a strong team player.

S7 *Explanation:* Agreement would suggest a considerate, conscientious employee.

S8 *Explanation:* Your approach to the management of others is under investigation here and agreement may suggest a lack of trust in the work of others.

S9 *Explanation:* Admitting to the possibility of not being able to cope is not a vote of confidence in yourself. Employers are looking for the candidate who rolls up his or her sleeves and helps clear up the mess when lots of things go wrong. They really do not want the added problem of staff declaring that they cannot cope.

S10 *Explanation:* Most employers would want you to agree with this statement as it shows sensitivity to the fact that colleagues might be offended by what was intended to be a humorous remark.

S11 *Explanation:* To agree most certainly suggests that you plan to prevail in everything you do. But it might be hard to place such a person in most working teams.

S12 *Explanation:* You might feel confident when you undertake familiar tasks but should not admit to feeling bored.

S13 *Explanation:* Agreement may be taken as a proactive, strategic approach or it might be looked at as risk-averse, which may or may not be a good thing.

S14 *Explanation:* Few employers would expect staff to adopt this stance and would prefer employees to treat customers and colleagues with tolerance irrespective of whether or not they were polite or considerate.

S15 *Explanation:* Your approach to people, relationships and effective communication is under examination here. In a customer-focused role it is likely that the employer would prefer agreement with this statement. To neither agree nor disagree might be appropriate in the case of a role in, for example, finance or banking when an auditable trail of compliance is required.

S16 *Explanation:* Whether or not you are happier in a team, few employers would be looking for an employee who admitted to not being able to rely on their own initiative.

S17 *Explanation:* Agreement suggests that you understand that the demands of your job and social life must be balanced. Disagreement risks the interpretation that you value your social life above your career.

S18 *Explanation:* Some employers are looking for candidates who are comfortable with, for example, the highly regulated culture in which they operate and they are seeking neither change nor innovation; others have a role in mind that demands a new outlook. How you answer this question will depend on the role for which you are applying.

S19 *Explanation:* Remember that these questions are not about your personal life, only your working life, and you should have no difficulty talking openly about your feelings relating to work.

S20 *Explanation:* It's good to express confidence in your own abilities and to portray yourself as someone who knows your own mind but be careful that you do not overdo this to the point of appearing arrogant or opinionated.

S21 *Explanation:* Where it is applicable, success may well require such a knowledge, but some organizations operate in a market in which success relies more on, for example, creativity, efficiency or relationships. Be sure to identify the secret of the success of the organization to which you are applying and use the findings of this research to shape your response to its questionnaire.

S22 *Explanation:* If it affects your ability to complete your work, then what you do in your own time may concern your employer. In some positions and for reasons of health and safety, the use of intoxicating substances the effect of which will still be felt at work could be taken as a breach of contract and grounds for disciplinary action.

S23 *Explanation:* Agreement risks the interpretation that you may be prone to paranoia!.

S24 *Explanation:* Your answers will depend on whether you want to work in a backroom role or a customer-facing role. Make sure your preference corresponds with the position for which you are applying.

S25 *Explanation:* You have to agree with a statement such as this or risk being identified as a non-team player, even a bit of a loner. Even agreement might risk the impression that you are less than proactive, and slow to take the initiative. But you just have to run that risk and agree.

S26 *Explanation:* Clever it may be, but few employers would find them appropriate.

S27 *Explanation:* Here once again your answer should depend on the company to which you are applying. Whether or not it is an advertising agency, if it serves multinationals then you should disagree. If it is a company that provides services to celebrities, then by all means agree.

S28 *Explanation:* Most employers would want their employees to disagree with this statement and approach every task with the same degree of care and attention.

S29 *Explanation:* You will not want to give the impression of being resistant to change, so it is wise to tread carefully. In many large and fast-developing organizations new initiatives abound.

S30 *Explanation:* Work is so different from our private life. This might be true in your private life but at work we all act differently. If you disclosed to a prospective employer that you might struggle to start conversations with colleagues or customers whom you do not know, then they would be likely to have reservations about your suitability for employment.

S31 *Explanation:* A no-blame culture is operated by some companies, so agree at your peril if you are completing the questionnaire as a part of your application to such a company.

S32 *Explanation:* A candidate for a professional position might well disagree with this. If candidates for other roles disagree, they might risk the impression of not being good team players.

S33 *Explanation:* Few employers would agree as the statement suggests that good manners should not always be displayed when at work.

S34 *Explanation:* Agreement suggests a very hands-on approach, except that it might be questioned, why ask to be copied into something you rarely have time to read? Agreement therefore risks the impression that you have difficulty trusting colleagues.

S35 *Explanation:* Competence would be expected in a professional role; in other roles it might be taken as lacking ambition. Decisiveness may well be desired by an organization with a relatively unstructured culture, but it might not appeal to more hierarchical organizations.

S36 *Explanation:* Agreement may risk the impression that you lack sensitivity to the needs of colleagues, but it will also stress a willingness to take risks and perhaps an entrepreneurial style.

S37 *Explanation:* Statements such as this are investigating your motivational approach. Many employers will assess staff against indicators that they may consider demanding and may be discouraged by a candidate who disagrees with this statement.

S38 *Explanation:* Disagreement might be expected from an all-rounder; agreement might be expected from a candidate applying for a role that demands focus, for example consultancy, or a candidate who prefers a focused style of working.

S39 *Explanation:* Agreeing will not score many points for ambition. The person who agrees is unlikely to be successful in an application for a graduate or managerial traineeship.

S40 *Explanation:* Agreement might well suit a results-orientated role and a company seeking a results-focused candidate, but make sure you are applying to an organization seeking such a person.

Attitudinal questionnaires to which there is most definitely a wrong answer

S1 *Answer:* Disagree. *Explanation:* Staff should be willing to help protect the property of their employer and doing so may in fact be an implicit condition of your contract of employment.

S2 *Answer:* Agree. *Explanation:* It would be unreasonable for an employer to expect you not to make any mistakes. Most would want you to inform your manager as soon as was practical and help put the consequences right.

S3 *Answer:* Disagree. *Explanation:* Be careful of negatives; it should be obvious to everyone these days that bad language is not appropriate in the workplace.

S4 *Answer:* Disagree. *Explanation:* Agreement with this statement would suggest you hold prejudices, ie preconceived opinions not based on experience or reason.

S5 *Answer:* Agree. *Explanation:* You may enjoy fiery relationships in your private life but there is no place for them at work, and blowing your top is not acceptable behaviour in any workplace.

S6 *Answer:* Agree or disagree. *Explanation:* If it is not a condition of your employment, then it is your own decision as to whether or not you might agree to such a request.

S7 *Answer:* Disagree. *Explanation:* A colleague who is off sick deserves support. The question of whether one has too great a workload should be treated as a separate matter and raised with one's line manager.

S8 *Answer:* Disagree. *Explanation:* Equality of opportunity is a matter taken very seriously by the vast majority of employers and it has a direct bearing on every job.

S9 *Answer:* Agree. *Explanation:* Being able to follow instructions in no way implies a lack of leadership. Every position in the world of work involves instruction from somewhere, be it shareholders to the CEO downwards. How could any employer employ someone who could not be comfortable when given instructions.

S10 *Answer:* Disagree. *Explanation:* Debate and discussion is an essential part of the process used in most places of work to arrive at good policy decisions. Inevitably this process involves differences of opinion, which need to be worked through in a responsible, professional manner.

Situational awareness tests

Situation 1: *Answer* 1C, 2B, 3B, 4C. *Explanation:* Response 1 is less than acceptable because if security tell you he is not an employee you may have caused a problem by leaving him unaccompanied in the building. Either response 2 or 3 is acceptable as it will result in you establishing whether or not he has the authority to be in the building.

Situation 2: *Answer* 1C, 2C, 3C, 4A. *Explanation:* Response 1 would be less than acceptable as it would involve you disclosing confidential information, response 2 is also less than acceptable because a team meeting is not the place to raise a matter of personal hygiene, response 3 would not be appropriate either because the issue has become one where it is affecting the working relations of your team. This leaves response 4 as the most appropriate.

Situation 3: *Answer* 1B, 2C, 3C, 4C. *Explanation:* Response 1 is acceptable but could be improved on if you undertook to act on the information urgently and inform the individual of the outcome. Response 2 is less than acceptable because you are most likely exceeding your authority to write saying that you agree the practice is dangerous. Responses 3 and 4 are less than acceptable because they are insufficiently proactive.

Situation 4: *Answer* 1B, 2C, 3A, 4C. *Explanation:* Response 1 is appropriate but not the most appropriate because although it shows leadership it lacks a collaborative approach. Response 2 might be appropriate under different circumstances; however, the partners lack morale and therefore may not respond positively to such a request. Response 3 is the most appropriate as it is both inclusive and mostly likely to be effective. Response 4 is less than acceptable because it fails to engage and collaborate.

Situation 5: *Answer* 1B, 2C, 3C, 4B. *Explanation:* Responses 2 and 3 are less than acceptable because they would result in the person using unacceptable language which others could hear. Either response 1 or 4 would succeed in dealing with the issue effectively while preventing bad language in the work place.

Situation 6: *Answer* 1C, 2C, 3C, 4A. *Explanation:* Responses 1, 2 and 3 are less than acceptable because they lack an inclusive team approach; response 1 is also not sufficiently proactive. Response 4 is likely to produce a way forward supported by all members of the team because they helped shape it.

Situation 7: *Answer* 1C, 2B, 3A, 4C. *Explanation:* Responses 1 and 4 are less than acceptable because they fail to inform people of the problems you have noticed. Response 2 is acceptable but it is less acceptable than response 3 because it does not provide an input for the individuals concerned.

Situation 8: *Answer* 1A, 2B, 3C, 4C. *Explanation:* Response 1 shows leadership and a strong proactive approach. Response 2 is acceptable in that your line manager may provide the needed leadership. Response 3 is less than acceptable because showing up at the meeting uninvited may inflame matters. Response 4 might be acceptable except that it misses the opportunity to start to address the partners dissatisfactions immediately.

Situation 9: *Answer* 1C, 2C, 3C, 4A. *Explanation:* The project has a life of one year and is about to enter the last quarter. If it is to achieve it overall targets, the final quarter must make up for all prior shortfall. For this reason the only appropriate response would be a red alert.

Situation 10: *Answer* 1B, 2C, 3B, 4B. *Explanation:* Response 1 is less than acceptable because it fails to ask for the male colleague's version of events, nor does it address his separate concern about the team meeting. Response 2 is also less than acceptable because it raises the issue of the inappropriate behaviour before the issue of the team meeting. Either response 3 or 4 should result in a satisfactory handling of both issues.

Chapter 3

A key skills diagnostic exercise

Diagnostic test

1   *Answer* $^3/_4$ = 0.75 = 75%.

2   *Answer* $^1/_5$ = 0.2 = 20%.

3   *Answer* $^3/_5$ = 0.6 = 60%.

4   *Answer* $^3/_8$ = 0.375 = 37.5%.

5   *Answer* $^1/_4$ = 0.25 = 25%.

6   *Answer* 3,530 JPY.   *Explanation:* 40 × 88.25 = 3,530.

7   *Answer* 4.4.   *Explanation:* 200 × 0.022 = 4.4.

8   *Answer* B 1 ZAR : 0.0846 GDP.   *Explanation:* Inverse means the oppose, so you must find the ZAR = GBP rate. Find this by dividing 1 by 11.82 and the closest suggested answer to this value is B, 0.0846.

9   *Answer* 0.714.   *Explanation:* 1 ÷ 1.4 = 0.714.

10   *Answer* 7 : 2.   *Explanation:* Express the ratio 14 : 4 in its lowest form = 7 : 2.

11   *Answer* £14.25.   *Explanation:* Total the sum of all sales and divide by the number of items to find the average.

12   *Answer* £27.75.   *Explanation:* 0.75 × 37 = 27.75.

13   *Answer* 840 centilitres.   *Explanation:* 9 litres = 900 centilitres ÷ 15 (14 + 1) = 60 × 14 = 840.

14   *Answer* D 40 cents.   *Explanation:* 6 ÷ 15 = $0.4 = 40 cents.

15   *Answer* 1,610.   *Explanation:* the wagon can hold 20,125 kg ÷ 12.5 = 1,610.

16   *Answer* $5,760.   *Explanation:* 1,200 × 30 = 36,000 discs at 0.16 = 5,760.

17   *Answer* 43.   *Explanation:* Total targets = 136 and sales so far = 93, which leaves 43 to realize the target.

18   *Answer* 84.   *Explanation:* An average of 52 means that the candidate failed each of the three papers by an average of 8 marks. So to improve the average to an average of 60 marks across four papers the candidate must gain $8 \times 3 = 24 + 60 = 84$ in the last paper.

19 *Answer* C £4,545. *Explanation:* 5,000 = 110%, 1% = 5000 ÷ 110 = approx 45.45 × 100 = 4,545.

20 *Answer* 14. *Explanation:* Add 3 each time.

21 *Answer* 576. *Explanation:* Multiply the previous figures in the sequence to find the next 12 x 48 = 576.

22 *Answer* 36. *Explanation:* The sequence is that of squared numbers (excluding 1), $2 \times 2 = 4$, $4 \times 4 = 16$, $5 \times 5 = 25$ and $6 \times 6 = 36$.

23 *Answer* 60%. *Explanation:* The cost price (£10) = 100%, £16 = 160% of the cost price, so the percentage profit = 60%.

24 *Answer* B, X = 1,800/3 + 1,000. *Explanation:* 1,800/3 = 600 + 1,000 = 1,600 (the sum X is to receive).

25 *Answer* A – 1, B – 4, C – 2, D – 3. *Explanation:* If a number is divided by 1 you find the reciprocal. For example 1 ÷ 25 = 0.04, etc. A familiarity with fundamentals such as reciprocals is a prerequisite to a good score in many numerical tests.

26 *Answer* 1 and 64. *Explanation:* A square number is a whole number raised to the power of 2, a cubed number is a whole number raised to the power of 3.

27 *Answer* C, 6. *Explanation:* The whole number factors of 18 are 1, 2, 3, 6, 9, 18.

28 *Answer* 30%. *Explanation:* The rating is an improper fraction of 1.5/5 which is equivalent to 3/10 or 30%.

29 *Answer* 5%. *Explanation:* 48 – 45 = 3 so find 3 as a percentage of the number of minutes in an hour. 3/60 = 1/20 = 0.05 or 5%.

30 *Answer* 150. *Explanation:* Add 1/3 + 5/12 = 9/12, leaving 3/12 over the last 3 days, 600 ÷ 12 = 50 × 3 = 150.

31 *Answer* 1,350. *Explanation:* Find 3/9 of 4,050. 4050 ÷ 9 = 450 × 3 = 1,350.

32   *Answer* E, 12. *Explanation:* Subtracting equation 1 from 2 gives $-a + b = 6$ or $b - a = 6$, multiply this by 2 gives $2b - 2a = 12$.

33   *Answer* $a = b$. *Explanation:* Zero multiplied by anything is zero, so b must be zero. This in turn means that a must be zero so $a = b$.

Sixty practice number problems

1	*Answer* 125.	**2**	*Answer* 48.
3	*Answer* 1,600 gallons.	**4**	*Answer* £268.80.
5	*Answer* $35.74.	**6**	*Answer* 105,000.
7	*Answer* 5 mph.	**8**	*Answer* £60,800.
9	*Answer* 1/20 kilogram.	**10**	*Answer* 120.
11	*Answer* $450.	**12**	*Answer* £198,000.
13	*Answer* $16.80.	**14**	*Answer* $4.50.
15	*Answer* £2.	**16**	*Answer* 62%.
17	*Answer* 1:49.	**18**	*Answer* 16%.
19	*Answer* $315.25.	**20**	*Answer* 28 pence.
21	*Answer* $42.50.	**22**	*Answer* 18 inches.
23	*Answer* £13,382.26.	**24**	*Answer* $200.
25	*Answer* £165.31.	**26**	*Answer* 60%.
27	*Answer* $350.	**28**	*Answer* £10.58.
29	*Answer* $350.	**30**	*Answer* £85.11.
31	*Answer* $84.	**32**	*Answer* £680.85.
33	*Answer* $30:$20.		
34	*Answer* A = 100, B = 500, C = 400.		
35	*Answer* 3:10.	**36**	*Answer* 15:6:4.
37	*Answer* 240.	**38**	*Answer* £2,448.
39	*Answer* £37.38.	**40**	*Answer* £2,400.

41	*Answer* 28 mph.	**42**	*Answer* $3\frac{1}{2}$ hours.
43	*Answer* 30 minutes.	**44**	*Answer* £80.19.
45	*Answer* 20 minutes.	**46**	*Answer* £22,368.
47	*Answer* 6,667 votes.	**48**	*Answer* 23.
49	*Answer* 1.	**50**	*Answer* $15,063.15.
51	*Answer* 14.	**52**	*Answer* 528.
53	*Answer* 504.	**54**	*Answer* 2.
55	*Answer* 1,500.	**56**	*Answer* 5.
57	*Answer* 128.	**58**	*Answer* 131.
59	*Answer* 243.	**60**	*Answer* 216.

Numerical test 1: Practice intermediate-level number problem test

1	*Answer* C.	**2**	*Answer* E.	**3**	*Answer* A.
4	*Answer* E.	**5**	*Answer* D.	**6**	*Answer* B.
7	*Answer* E.	**8**	*Answer* A.	**9**	*Answer* F.
10	*Answer* D.	**11**	*Answer* C.	**12**	*Answer* D.
13	*Answer* B.	**14**	*Answer* C.	**15**	*Answer* D.
16	*Answer* E.	**17**	*Answer* A.	**18**	*Answer* C.
19	*Answer* B.	**20**	*Answer* F.	**21**	*Answer* C.
22	*Answer* F.	**23**	*Answer* A.		

24 *Answer* A, 2 hours.   *Explanation:* The two people can fill the truck twice in 8 hours, so they will take 4 hours to fill it and 2 hours to half-fill it.

25 *Answer* 7 and 21.   *Explanation:* The first number = 3 × the second, so first number = $3x$ and $3x + x = 28$, so $4x = 28$, $x = 7$; the numbers are 7 and (3 × 7) 21.

26 *Answer* 600.   *Explanation:* 492 gallons represents 82% of the original amount of fuel. You must find 100%; 1% = 492 ÷ 82 = 6, so 100% = 600.

27 *Answer* 667. *Explanation:* Find the average to calculate the sum. There are 40 – 18 + 1 numbers in the range (you have to add the 1, otherwise you are a number short) = 23 numbers; the average is 18 + 40 = 58 ÷ 2 = 29; the sum = 29 × 23 = 667.

28 *Answer* 38, 39, 40. *Explanation:* Make x the first number; $x + (x + 1) + (x + 2) = 117$, so $3x + 3 = 117$, so $3x = 114$, $114 ÷ 3 = x$, $x = 38$, therefore the numbers are 38, 39, 40.

29 *Answer* 24 minutes. *Explanation:* $28 = 6x$ walking + $1x$ cycling; $28 ÷ 7 = 4$, $1 × 4 = 4$ minutes cycling, 24 minutes walking.

30 *Answer* 33. *Explanation:* $99 – 67 + 1$ (we add the 1, otherwise we fail to count 67) = 33.

Numerical test 2: Practice intermediate-level sequencing test

1 *Answer* 59. **2** *Answer* 12. **3** *Answer* 44.

4 *Answer* 99. **5** *Answer* 40. **6** *Answer* 92.

7 *Answer* 62. **8** *Answer* 09. **9** *Answer* 08.

10 *Answer* 10. **11** *Answer* 12. **12** *Answer* 08.

13 *Answer* 19. **14** *Answer* 14. **15** *Answer* 11.

16 *Answer* 50. **17** *Answer* 20. **18** *Answer* 40.

19 *Answer* 60. **20** *Answer* 06. **21** *Answer* 10.

22 *Answer* 10. *Explanation:* The sequence is 2, 4, 6, 8, 10 but the 4 and 8 have been presented in a misleading way.

23 *Answer* 31.

24 *Answer* 81.

25 *Answer* 24 to give 244. *Explanation:* To find the sequence you have to go through two steps. First, work out the increase between the numbers, ie $10 – 4 = 6$, $28 – 10 = 18$, $82 – 28 = 54$. Now take this new sequence, 6, 18, 54; here each new number is three times the previous number and extending the series we get 6, 18, 54, 162, 486. The number XX4 can now be found, as XX4 − 82 = 162, ie XX4 = 162 + 82 = 244. Or 730 − XX4 = 486, ie XX4 = 730 − 486 = 244.

26 *Answer* 53. *Explanation:* Again, to find the sequence you have to go through two steps. First, add together the grouped numbers 1 + 1 = 2, 1 + 2 = 3, etc, which gives the series 2, 3, 5, 7. This is a sequence of prime numbers, which can be extended to give 2, 3, 5, 7, 11, 13, and then working backwards gives the answer.

Numerical test 3: Intermediate data interpretation practice test

Q1	*Answer* 7.	**Q2**	*Answer* A.
Q3	*Answer* B.	**Q4**	*Answer* 1.
Q5	*Answer* C.	**Q6**	*Answer* A.
Q7	*Answer* B.	**Q8**	*Answer* 3.
Q9	*Answer* B.	**Q10**	*Answer* A.
Q11	*Answer* D.	**Q12**	*Answer* 3.
Q13	*Answer* A.	**Q14**	*Answer* C.
Q15	*Answer* B.	**Q16**	*Answer* 2.
Q17	*Answer* C.	**Q18**	*Answer* A.
Q19	*Answer* C.	**Q20**	*Answer* 1.
Q21	*Answer* B and C.	**Q22**	*Answer* A, B and D.
Q23	*Answer* C.	**Q24**	*Answer* B and D.
Q25	*Answer* A and B.	**Q26**	*Answer* A, C and E.
Q27	*Answer* B.	**Q28**	*Answer* B, D and F.
Q29	*Answer* E.	**Q30**	*Answer* A, C and E.

Numerical test 4: Practice intermediate-level data interpretation test

1	Answer 1.	**2**	Answer 3.
3	Answer 4.	**4**	Answer 3.
5	Answer 1.	**6**	Answer 4.
7	Answer 3.	**8**	Answer 2.
9	Answer 3.	**10**	Answer 4.
11	Answer 1.	**12**	Answer 1.
13	Answer 3.	**14**	Answer 1.
15	Answer 4.	**16**	Answer 1.

17 Answer 3. *Explanation:* 72% + 12% (fire damage) = 84%, 100% − 84% = 16% of claims are fraudulent; 16% of 2,500 = 400.

18 *Answer* Cannot tell. *Explanation:* We know that 12% of all claims = ratio 3:25 but we do not know the percentage of genuine claims and we are not provided with enough information to establish the number of genuine claims, so we cannot answer the question.

19 *Answer* 1. *Explanation:* Calculate 12% of 7,000 = 840; 420,000 ÷ 840 = 500.

20 *Answer* 4. *Explanation:* 20/100 × 360 = 72 degrees.

21 *Answer* y. *Explanation:* The horizontal axis is called the x axis and the vertical the y axis.

22 *Answer* 3. *Explanation:* The average wage increased 200 cents over the period illustrated and the trade value from manufacturing for export fell by $9bn over the same period. 9bn = 9,000 million ÷ 200 = 90 ÷ 2 = 45 million per cent, loss.

23 *Answer* 4. *Explanation:* This information is not provided.

24 *Answer* 4. *Explanation:* 19 = 5%, 19 ÷ 5 = 3.8 × 100 = 380.

25 *Answer* 3. *Explanation:* $^{10}/_{150} = ^1/_{15} \times 360 = 24$.

Numerical test 5: Advanced data interpretation practice test

Q1 *Answer* 0.02. *Explanation:* aps = savings/income = 8/400 = 0.02.

Q2 *Answer* 0.05. *Explanation:* Total both the saving and incomes for the three months and divide saving/income= 145/2900 = 0.05.

Q3 *Answer* $20. *Explanation:* Calculate the aps for both the original level of income and the increased level = 0.05 × 1,100 = 55, 0.05 × 1,500 = 75. Subtract the original level from the increased level to establish how much more people would save: 55 − 75 = 20.

Q4 *Answer* Country 2. *Explanation:* Country 1 aps = 35/700 = 0.05, country 2 = 50/800 = 0.065, country 3 is given as 0.03.

Q5 *Answer* True. *Explanation:* The new machine is twice as fast as the old, 50 minutes ÷ 2 = 25, 1,000,000 ÷ 25 = 40,000.

Q6 *Answer* False. *Explanation:* We are told that twenty-four billion pounds is invested in Premium Bonds and in the past 10 years the number of bonds in the draw has increased sevenfold, but 24 ÷ 7 ≠ 4.

Q7 *Answer* Cannot tell. *Explanation:* A billion can be defined as either a thousand million or a million million. The first of these definitions is the more common, but strictly speaking you cannot tell, given the information contained in the passage.

Q8 *Answer* 5. *Explanation:* It is clear from the opening balance that the company would require access to external cash for five out of the six months covered by the cash-flow forecast.

Q9 *Answer* 40%. *Explanation:* In $000 sales, total 105 and direct costs 42. 42/105 = 0.4 × 100 = 40.

Q10 *Answer* 3:7. *Explanation:* In total, $18,000 is spent on net wages and $42,000 on direct costs, so you must express 18:42, which reduces to 3:7.

Q11 *Answer* $2,200. *Explanation:* To find the opening balance, add the monthly + or – to the previous opening balance, = 1.6 + 0.6 = 2.2 or $2,200.

Q12 *Answer* $4,500. *Explanation:* First calculate the percentage of 3,000 (net wages) that NI and pensions represent. But notice that the figure of 2.7 NI/pensions related to three months' net wages, so calculate 2.7/9 = 0.3 × 100 = 30%. Now calculate 30% of 24,000 (3 × 8,000 monthly net wages) = 7,200 and finally subtract the original 2,700 to get $4,500 a quarter.

Q13 *Answer* False. *Explanation:* The passage states that the government wants 50% of people aged 18–30 to go to university, but not all of them will study for a foundation degree.

Q14 *Answer* Cannot tell. *Explanation:* The passage provides no information about the motivational qualities of successful students on foundation degrees, beyond the statement that they are not for the faint-hearted.

Q15 *Answer* Cannot tell. *Explanation:* The passage states that there are 20,000 people already doing foundation degrees and that half of all the courses available have 50 or more students enrolled, but from this we cannot calculate or infer that there are 200 courses with 50 or more students enrolled.

Q16 *Answer* 250m. *Explanation:* Calculate 4% of 1,000 and add it to 12% of 1,750m = 40 + 210 = $250m.

Q17 *Answer* False. *Explanation:* You are only given gross profit and not the cost of sales, so you cannot calculate the value of sales for 2005 or 2006.

Q18 *Answer* 45m. *Explanation:* Calculate 57% of 1,000 = 570, 30% of 1,750 = 525, minus 525 from 570 = 45. Express your answer in millions of dollars.

Q19 *Answer* E. *Explanation:* Gross profit means in this context the difference between revenue and the cost of goods sold. This definition is not given. A defines gross revenue, B would be an acceptable definition of net profit, C = gross profit margin, D = gross receipt.

Q20 *Answer* 1:10. *Explanation:* You have previously calculated the two-year contribution of coal as 250m. Subtract this from the two-year gross profit total, 2,750 – 250 = 2,500. Now express 250 as a ratio to 2,500 in its simplest form = 1:10.

Q21 *Answer* False. *Explanation:* Overall the chance is 1 in 4, but in an urban school the chances are greater. The gender of the child will also change the odds.

Q22 *Answer* True. *Explanation:* The ratio for infections of girls and boys is not dependent on the type of school. There might be more infections found in the urban school but the ratio would remain 3:1.

Q23 *Answer* False. *Explanation:* The passage states that lice cannot fly or jump and that infections are more common in girls because their play tends to involves close head contact. It cannot be inferred from these assertions, however, that lice crawl from one head to another, because infections might be transmitted in another way – for example, by the transfer of eggs and not adult lice.

Chapter 4

One hundred and thirty-five practice questions

1	*Answer* C.	2	*Answer* B.
3	*Answer* C.	4	*Answer* A.
5	*Answer* A.	6	*Answer* A.
7	*Answer* B.	8	*Answer* B.
9	*Answer* A.	10	*Answer* C.
11	*Answer* C.	12	*Answer* A.
13	*Answer* C.	14	*Answer* A.
15	*Answer* D.	16	*Answer* A.
17	*Answer* C.	18	*Answer* A.

19 *Answer* C.

20 *Answer* A.

21 *Answer* B.

22 *Answer* B and C.

23 *Answer* A.

24 *Answer* A and B.

25 *Answer* A.   *Explanation:* Note that while '1960's' is often seen in print, this is not correct.

26 *Answer* D.

27 *Answer* B.

28 *Answer* D.

29 *Answer* C.

30 *Answer* C.

31 *Answer* C.

32 *Answer* A.

33 *Answer* B, F and G.

34 *Answer* A, C, D, E and F.

35 *Answer* A.

36 *Answer* B.

37 *Answer* A.

38 *Answer* C.

39 *Answer* A.

40 *Answer* B.

41 *Answer* B.

42 *Answer* C.

43 *Answer* C.

44 *Answer* C.

45 *Answer* Complimentary.

46 *Answer* Effect.

47 *Answer* Continual.

48 *Answer* Advice.

49 *Answer* All ready.

50 *Answer* Among.

51 *Answer* Into.

52 *Answer* No word required.

53 *Answer* Flaunt.

54 *Answer* Take.

55 *Answer* from.

56 *Answer* Fewer.

57 *Answer* Farther.

58 *Answer* I.

59 *Answer* Lying.

Word link practice questions

64 *Answer* golf club.

65 *Answer* ship hospital.

66 *Answer* manage regulate.

67 *Answer* top bottom.

68 *Answer* king palace.

69 *Answer* construct retire.

70 *Answer* horse bench.

71 *Answer* agree dispute.

72 *Answer* emperor empire.

73 *Answer* horse hair.

74 *Answer* car petrol.

75 *Answer* light dark.

76 *Answer* anarchy order.

77 *Answer* red green.

78 *Answer* Asia Europe.

79 *Answer* competent defective.

80 *Answer* sketches appraises.

81 *Answer* west east.

82 *Answer* blockage conclusion.

83 *Answer* cloth leather.

84 *Answer* paper note.

85 *Answer* untimely disgraceful.

86 *Answer* metre foot.

87 *Answer* strong experienced.

88 *Answer* genial affable.

89 *Answer* work deviate.

90 *Answer* compliant defiant.

91 *Answer* mystic devotee.

92 *Answer* obfuscation encyclopedist.

93 *Answer* perfection gluttonous.

94 *Answer* behaviourism psychology.

95 *Answer* abundance profusion.

Word swap

96 *Answer* securing aimed.

97 *Answer* line press.

98 *Answer* equal person.

99 *Answer* London association.

100 *Answer* grade range.

101 *Answer* kicking back.

102 *Answer* things naming.

103 *Answer* subject paragraph.

104 *Answer* sold made.

105 *Answer* private consultants.

106 *Answer* worried pledged.

107 *Answer* 30,00   50,000.

108 *Answer* impressive predictable.

109 *Answer* grandfather lord.

110 *Answer* ancient hard.

Sentence sequencing questions

112 *Answer*	1	3	4	2		**113** *Answer*	1	3	4	2
114 *Answer*	1	4	3	2		**115** *Answer*	3	1	2	4
116 *Answer*	2	1	3	4		**117** *Answer*	2	4	1	3
118 *Answer*	2	4	3	1		**119** *Answer*	3	2	1	4
120 *Answer*	4	1	3	2		**121** *Answer*	3	2	1	4
122 *Answer*	2	4	1	3		**123** *Answer*	3	1	4	2
124 *Answer*	3	2	4	1		**125** *Answer*	3	2	4	1
126 *Answer*	3	2	1	4		**127** *Answer*	2	4	3	1
128 *Answer*	4	2	3	1		**129** *Answer*	3	1	2	4
130 *Answer*	2	4	1	3		**131** *Answer*	3	2	1	4
132 *Answer*	3	2	4	1		**133** *Answer*	4	1	3	2
134 *Answer*	2	1	4	3		**135** *Answer*	3	4	1	2

Test 1: Practice test of English usage

1 *Answer* C.	**2** *Answer* A.	**3** *Answer* No error.
4 *Answer* A.	**5** *Answer* A.	**6** *Answer* D.
7 *Answer* D.	**8** *Answer* B.	**9** *Answer* C.
10 *Answer* D.	**11** *Answer* A.	**12** *Answer* B.
13 *Answer* B.	**14** *Answer* D.	**15** *Answer* A.
16 *Answer* C.	**17** *Answer* C.	**18** *Answer* A.
19 *Answer* A.	**20** *Answer* D.	**21** *Answer* B.
22 *Answer* A.	**23** *Answer* D.	**24** *Answer* D.
25 *Answer* A.		

Test 2: Practice intermediate-level critical reasoning test

1   *Answer* Not possible to say.

2   *Answer* False.

3   *Answer* False.

4   *Answer* Not possible to say.

5   *Answer* Not possible to say.

6   *Answer* Not possible to say.

7   *Answer* True.

8   *Answer* False.

9   *Answer* True.

10   *Answer* False.

11   *Answer* True.

12   *Answer* True.

13   *Answer* Not possible to say.

14   *Answer* False.

15   *Answer* Not possible to say.

16   *Answer* Not possible to say.

17   *Answer* False.

18   *Answer* True.

19   *Answer* Not possible to say.

20   *Answer* A incorrect B correct.

21   *Answer* A incorrect B incorrect.

22   *Answer* A correct B incorrect.

23   *Answer* A incorrect B correct.

24   *Answer* A correct B correct.

25   *Answer* A correct B correct.

26   *Answer* A incorrect B incorrect.

27   *Answer* A correct B correct.

28   *Answer* A correct B incorrect.

29   *Answer* A correct B correct.

Test 3: Practice intermediate-level critical reasoning test

Q1 *Answer* True.   **Q2** *Answer* Cannot tell.

Q3 *Answer* True.   **Q4** *Answer* True.

Q5 *Answer* Cannot tell.   **Q6** *Answer* Cannot tell.

Q7 *Answer* False.   **Q8** *Answer* True.

Q9 *Answer* Cannot tell.   **Q10** *Answer* Cannot tell.

Q11 *Answer* True.   **Q12** *Answer* Cannot tell.

Q13 *Answer* True.   **Q14** *Answer* True.

Q15 *Answer* False.   *Explanation:* Only 16 per cent did.

Q16 *Answer* True.   **Q17** *Answer* True.

Q18 *Answer* Cannot tell. **Q19** *Answer* True.

Q20 *Answer* False.   **Q21** *Answer* False.

Q22 *Answer* False.   **Q23** *Answer* True.

Q24 *Answer* Cannot tell.

Q25 *Answer* False.   *Explanation:* 19 per cent raised the price.

Q26 *Answer* Cannot tell.

Q27 *Answer* True.

Q28 *Answer* False.   *Explanation:* The figures are unconnected, so it must be coincidence.

Q29 *Answer* Not enough information.

Q30 *Answer* Action required.

Q31 *Answer* No action required.

Q32 *Answer* No action required.

Q33 *Answer* No action required.

Q34 *Answer* Not enough information.

Q35 *Answer* Not enough information.

Q36 *Answer* No action required.

Test 4: Practice advanced-level reading comprehension and critical reasoning test

Q1 *Answer* False. *Explanation:* The passage describes the design of the nose and wing as important in the best designs that achieve the longest flights.

Q2 *Answer* Cannot tell. *Explanation:* The passage does not touch on the subject of a paper plane's performance outside.

Q3 *Answer* True. *Explanation:* The term used in the passage is 'cambered', which means slightly arched or convex.

Q4 *Answer* False. *Explanation:* The passage states that a paper plane should not be made with these features; it does not state that it is not possible to make such a plane. If one is made, it does not weaken the case made within the passage.

Q5 *Answer* True. *Explanation:* A careful reading of the passage will confirm this.

Q6 *Answer* Cannot tell. *Explanation:* The passage states that the scientists are drawn from nine countries across every populated continent but it does not say what sample they will use to undertake their study.

Q7 *Answer* False. *Explanation:* Our genetic differences explain our propensity for particular diseases, not the extent to which we are genetically identical.

Q8 *Answer* False. *Explanation:* This point is explicitly stated in the passage, so it is false to say that it can be inferred.

Q9 *Answer* C.	**Q10** *Answer* C.	**Q11** *Answer* B.
Q12 *Answer* B.	**Q13** *Answer* D.	**Q14** *Answer* C.
Q15 *Answer* A.	**Q16** *Answer* D.	**Q17** *Answer* C.
Q18 *Answer* C.	**Q19** *Answer* C.	**Q20** *Answer* B.
Q21 *Answer* A.	**Q22** *Answer* B.	**Q23** *Answer* B.

Test 5: Practice advanced-level reading comprehension and critical reasoning test

Q1 *Answer* False. *Explanation:* The passage does not state that people are switching from private cars to, for example, public transport, allowing you to infer that people will be switching to trains as one form of public transport.

Q2 *Answer* Cannot tell. *Explanation:* It is true that the passage concludes that travellers face overcrowding, slower journey times and in some states closures, but the passage does not mention higher fares.

Q3 *Answer* False. *Explanation:* The issue is the small amount of investment in both road and rail transport and is not limited only to the railway.

Q4 *Answer* True. *Explanation:* A reading of the passage shows that the problems are already chronic in these areas and the problems are bottlenecks, congestion and overcrowding.

Q5 *Answer* True. *Explanation:* You should not answer 'Cannot tell' here. The question is offering the statement that 'at home European travellers face a bleak future of overcrowding and congestion' as a summary of the passage's conclusion, and your task is to decide whether that is a valid summary or not (and it is).

Q6 *Answer* True. *Explanation:* The main theme of the passage is the failure of bright children from low-income homes to achieve the same grades as bright children from high-income families.

Q7 *Answer* False. *Explanation:* The passage does cover the findings of the research but it does not comment on any debate that ensued.

Q8 *Answer* True. *Explanation:* It is said in the first sentence that 'recent research has provided further stark evidence of the educational apartheid…'.

Q9 *Answer* False. *Explanation:* The passage reports in a journalistic manner; it is not an unreliable source, so is not anecdotal, and it is written in the third person, so cannot be described as dogmatic.

Q10 *Answer* False. *Explanation:* This cannot be inferred because the passage provides no information on the role parental encouragement and home resources may or may not play in realizing potential.

Q11 *Answer* Cannot tell. *Explanation:* The passage does not provide details of the observed squid, only that the species is believed to reach that length.

Q12 *Answer* False. *Explanation:* It is stated in the passage that this is what the research reasoned, so it cannot be inferred from the passage.

Q13 *Answer* True. *Explanation:* The approach made towards the bait by the squid was vigorous, as the squid is described as 'shooting out'.

Q14 *Answer* True. *Explanation:* The passage describes the filming as the first of the squid in its natural habitat and that it occurred at a depth of 1 kilometre.

Q15 *Answer* Cannot tell. *Explanation:* The passage does not detail what sperm whales eat. It is stated that giant squid have been found in the stomach of whales, but which type of whale was not specified.

Q16 *Answer* True. *Explanation:* This is clear from a reading of the passage.

Q17 *Answer* True. *Explanation:* The passage does not state the objective for punishment but it states that the system is failing because of the high rate of reoffending after or even during punishment.

Q18 *Answer* Cannot tell. *Explanation:* From the information given, we do not know why offenders are willing to risk being caught and punished again, and we cannot infer why. The reason may be, for example, that they are convinced they will not get caught, rather than a lack of fear of the consequences.

Q19 *Answer* False. *Explanation:* The reason stated for abandoning these programmes is overcrowding and not that they are ineffective.

Q20 *Answer* False. *Explanation:* It is not clear from a reading of the passage that we need to find alternative solutions.

Q21 *Answer* True.   *Explanation:* No adverse association means no harm, and the author would agree that a diet of fibre does not bring an increase in risk.

Q22 *Answer* Cannot tell.   *Explanation:* The passage provides no information on the relationship between a diet high in fibre and other diseases such as heart disease.

Q23 *Answer* False.   *Explanation:* It is stated in the passage that 'it so happens that people with high-fibre diets eat less red meat and milk products than people with low-fibre diets. People who eat lots of fibre also tend to enjoy a lifestyle with many other factors that may confer a lower risk of contracting colorectal cancer'.

Q24 *Answer* True.   *Explanation:* It is stated in the passage that 'a propensity for the disease is also known to be inherited'.

Q25 *Answer* False.   *Explanation:* In this case an inverse association means that as the amount of fibre consumed increases, the occurrence of colon cancer should decrease, and the author would not agree that such an inverse association exists.

Q26 *Answer* False.   *Explanation:* It is clear that the statement does not support the main theme of the passage, which is that a return to nuclear power is being considered because so many countries are failing to reduce their CO_2 emissions.

Q27 *Answer* True.   *Explanation:* If renewable sources already existed, the case for a temporary return to nuclear power would be greatly weakened.

Q28 *Answer* False.   *Explanation:* They are not contradictory, as the electricity generating stage of nuclear power's life may not be when it is far from clean.

Q29 *Answer* Cannot tell.   *Explanation:* The passage makes the case that, in the longer term, alternatives hold the answer to global warming, but it does not state which alternatives these might be. So, it is not possible to tell whether wind, wave and tidal power hold the answer.

Q30 *Answer* False.   *Explanation:* This is not explicitly stated in the passage.